100 Low Sodium Recipes

(For Big Appetites!)

Mark Knoblauch PhD

Kiremma Press

Disclaimer: This book is not intended and must not be used as a substitute for the medical advice of licensed medical professionals. The reader should regularly consult his or her physician in any matter relating to his/her health and particularly with respect to any symptoms that may require diagnosis of a medical attention. The author makes no guarantees concerning the level of success you may experience by following the advice and strategies contained in this book, and you accept the risk that results will differ for each individual. The use of this book implies your acceptance of this disclaimer. Furthermore, this cookbook in no way provides any warranty, express or implied, towards the content of its recipes. It is the reader's responsibility to determine the value and quality of any recipe or instructions provided for food preparation and to determine the nutritional value, safety of the preparation instructions, potential for food allergies, etc. Many factors can affect how a recipe turns out – cooking temperatures or time, humidity, altitude, climate, different appliances, experience, substitutions, etc. The recipes presented are intended for entertainment and/or informational purposes and for use by persons having the appropriate technical skill, at their own discretion and risk.

ISBN: 978-1-7333210-3-7

To my wife and kids, who have patiently sat through the development of multiple (bad) iterations of my recipes before finally finding a version we can all enjoy

Table of Contents

Introduction

Welcome to *100 Low-sodium Recipes (For Big Appetites)!* Given that you have acquired this cookbook, I would venture to guess that either you or someone you love has decided to embark on the low-sodium lifestyle. You read that right – it's a *lifestyle,* not just 'a diet'. Diets are all about food and in most cases are for a defined period of time, such as until a weight-loss goal is met. A lifestyle change is more comprehensive and involves ongoing education as well as healthy choices that can go on for an indefinite amount of time. As a result of their all-encompassing nature, lifestyle changes tend to be more comprehensive and can involve more aspects than a traditional diet. Like any lifestyle change, to be successful in a low-sodium lifestyle requires adherence on your part as well as those around you. The process can certainly come with a bit of frustration and will likely involve a few cravings along the way, but the rewards that come with being successful can have immense health benefits.

For some, the decision to embark on the low-sodium lifestyle may have occurred seemingly through force – such as being diagnosed with a medical condition that requires a reduction in sodium intake. Others may be taking on the lifestyle change due to a conscious decision to consume less sodium in order to improve their health. Regardless of your underlying reason, here you are. Though a low-sodium lifestyle may seem daunting at first, rest assured that it is both possible and quite rewarding. I can say this because I'm a practitioner myself.

My own reason for taking the low-sodium journey, as we'll outline in detail later, stems from being diagnosed with a medical condition nearly a decade ago that is intimately tied to sodium intake. Since making the switch from a traditional diet to a low sodium diet there have certainly been a few bumps in the road when trying to learn about what foods I can have, but the payoff of significantly better health makes it all worthwhile. Although there are some *sources* of food that I choose to live without because of their sodium content – such as the majority of traditional fast food items as well as many store-bought prepared meals – I am still able to enjoy those same types of foods when prepared as their modified, 'homemade' versions. You'll likely learn that a low sodium lifestyle does take some adapting on your part when it comes to food choices and there will undoubtedly be a learning curve, but if you go in with the mindset of it being a lifestyle change and not simply a 'diet', I think you'll find it much easier to be successful.

Why are we here?

So why write a cookbook when a wealth of recipes can easily be found on the internet? Well, there are several reasons for this. First, I don't think that an individual can truly understand low-sodium cooking unless they understand sodium itself. Therefore, I didn't want to simply put a collection of recipes together in order to say that I wrote a cookbook. Rather, I wanted to help you strengthen your *understanding* of sodium, so I have included relevant information specific to what sodium is, why our body needs it, and why it's so prevalent in our food. Helping you understand how our bodies interact with sodium can allow you to find a happy medium between recognizing that sodium is essential for survival and being aware of the potential health consequences when sodium is consumed in excess. In short, I wanted to write a cookbook that doesn't simply imply *eat less sodium*. Instead, I wanted my cookbook to include information specific to *why* sodium is important but does not necessarily need to be consumed in the amounts that a traditional diet supplies us.

My second reason for writing a cookbook is because in most cases, the format used for cookbooks is frustrating to me. Not frustrating in such a way that the author did anything incorrectly – in fact, they almost always write their recipes using the accepted format for a cookbook: a personal story about how the recipe impacts them or why the recipe means so much to them, a step-by-step narrative of how to prepare the recipe, then an overview of the recipe's nutrition information *per serving.* This last aspect is something that actually spurred me to write my own cookbook on my own terms. As someone who considers himself a 'big eater' and is very picky about sodium content, seeing a *Spaghetti with Meat Sauce* recipe that lists an 8oz serving as having 460mg of sodium just isn't practical for me. In fact, a couple of issues arise in using this recipe format. First of all – how much is 8oz of a prepared spaghetti recipe? While putting some spaghetti and sauce on my plate I could guess, of course, as to how much of the recipe could fit into approximately one cup (i.e. 8oz), but I'm more practical in my consumption habits. It's easier for me to assess the proportion (e.g. half, one-third, etc.) of how much of a recipe I consumed rather than estimate some arbitrary serving size. Secondly, I'm 6'2", 215lbs. Established serving sizes are so impractical for big-eaters like me that by the time we feel full, we've eaten an embarrassing number of servings along with an excessive amount of sodium that didn't initially seem so bad when listed 'per serving'.

To address these issues, I wanted to design a low-sodium cookbook that was more transparent about sodium content. Specifically, I wanted to develop and outline recipes which include the total sodium content for the *entire dish* rather than per serving. Doing so would allow consumers to calculate their sodium content based on how much of a dish they consumed rather than trying to calculate how many servings their helping was comprised of. Therefore, recipes in this cookbook are formatted to allow you to make your own sodium intake estimations based on how much of each recipe you consume. For example, if the prepared lasagna recipe is cut into 6 sections and you consume two of them, you could simply divide the dish's total sodium content by a value of 3 to figure out how much sodium you consumed. To me, this is much easier than trying to determine how many 8-ounce servings made up the two lasagna sections that you ate. Similarly, in those cases where you're able to consume the entire prepared recipe from this book (it happens, let me assure you), the sodium content is already established for you with no calculation needed.

The third reason I wanted to write a cookbook is because I wanted a better way to provide you the nutritional information specific to each recipe. In my mind, there's no better way to do that than to replicate the Nutrition Facts label. Anyone on a special diet or conscious of calories is likely familiar with the Nutrition Facts label found on the back of almost every food package. My own low-sodium lifestyle is intimately tied to the Nutrition Facts label, and it has been my lifeline for making food and ingredient decisions. Therefore, I wanted to develop a cookbook that includes not only the sodium content for the entire prepared recipe but also displays that sodium content (along with other nutritional information) on the familiar Nutrition Facts label.

Design Aspects

In this book you'll find 100 recipes that I have developed or modified over the past decade which allow me to eat the amount of food my family and I enjoy at mealtime. Originally, my thoughts wavered about whether I should create a massive, comprehensive low-sodium cookbook with hundreds of recipes. Or perhaps a cookbook with a threshold of less than 1,000mg per recipe. I soon realized, though, that sticking to these design criteria wouldn't accurately represent my own low-sodium cooking style. Furthermore, to fulfill those criteria I would have to scour the internet to find untested recipes just to meet a predefined recipe quota. To me, that would violate the ethics of recipe sharing, and I certainly wouldn't feel honest as a cookbook author in including recipes that hadn't been modified to my liking first. And the more I thought about it, adding recipes just to make a thicker cookbook would stray from my original intent of creating a cookbook for 'big eaters'. Consequently, I decided not to put in 'every' recipe that I use. I didn't include my recipes for guacamole or salsa, nor my favorite popcorn recipe (pop the corn in canola oil then top with melted unsalted butter, salt substitute, and a sprinkle of parmesan cheese) or my version of scrambled eggs (4 beaten eggs, 1 tbsp milk, ½ tsp vanilla extract). And I didn't include overly-simple recipes like toast or oatmeal, or even my two-ingredient (instant rice and butter) or three-ingredient (instant rice, ground beef, black pepper) recipes despite their simplicity. Instead, I wanted to focus on ample-sized entrées, throw in a few of my favorite sides that can go along with those entrées, and also include a couple of unique breakfast items and desserts to allow you some variety.

In short, what you'll find in this cookbook are 100 recipes that have become the staple meal selection in our house. These recipes were developed over time and are based on the individual preferences of myself and my family. You and your family may have quite different taste preferences, so if at any point you come across a recipe in this cookbook that doesn't quite fit your liking, do what I did – modify it! You might find a need to add your own unique set of spices, reduce the meat content, or perhaps even add a little salt to meet your personal preferences. By all means – do so! You'll already have the recipe's sodium content outlined for you on the Nutrition Facts label, so simply adjust the original sodium of the recipe to meet your modifications.

Although this cookbook focuses on providing low-sodium recipes with an ample amount of food, some recipes (e.g. Cottage Pie – 2,080mg of sodium) might appear at first glance to have a relatively high sodium content. When you factor in the total quantity of food in those recipes, though, you'll find that it is not realistic to expect that the entire recipe will be consumed in one sitting. Therefore, the higher per-recipe sodium amount can be viewed more favorably given that it will likely be spread across two or more meals. To highlight the sodium content of recipes in this book versus traditional recipes, let's compare my Cottage Pie recipe versus what you can find in a traditional Cottage Pie recipe available online. For comparison, I found two recipes prepared in a 9"x13" baking dish similar to mine and calculated the total sodium content for the dish by multiplying the sodium amount per serving by the number of servings. For further comparison's sake I also included the Cottage/Shepherd's Pie recipe from a couple of major restaurant chains, though it should be noted that the total prepared amount differs significantly:

Source	Quantity	Total Sodium Content
This cookbook	Full recipe – 9"x13" dish	2,080mg
Internet Recipe A	Full recipe – 9"x13" dish	5,448mg
Internet Recipe B	Full recipe – 9"x13" dish	9,296mg
Major Restaurant Chain "A"	Serving	2,960mg
Major Restaurant Chain "B"	Per 1 cup serving	720mg

As you can see, even though the Cottage Pie recipe from this book has over 2,000mg of sodium, it is still significantly less than traditional recipes as well as restaurant portions. Despite a similar amount of food between recipes (i.e. assembly of the pie in a 9"x13" baking dish), the two internet-based recipe examples have a 160-346% higher sodium content than what you'll find in the recipe from this cookbook. As for the restaurant dishes, restaurant "A" lists their Cottage Pie sodium content 'as prepared' and has nearly 3,000mg of sodium, yet represents a much smaller recipe quantity than what you'll find in this cookbook. Restaurant "B" lists a sodium value of 720mg 'per 1 cup serving'. Given that there are on average 12 cups per 9"x13" baking dish, if prepared in the same quantity represented in this cookbook, restaurant "B" would have a total sodium content of over 8,500mg.

What's NOT in this Cookbook

In having discussed several of the unique aspects of this cookbook so far, I think it's important to also outline what's *not* in this cookbook. While I certainly recognize that cookbooks have a traditional format that many users often prefer, I decided to direct this cookbook's efforts toward providing an educational overview of sodium while also providing practical, low-sodium recipes that provide ample amounts of food. Therefore, you won't find recipes introduced with heartwarming anecdotes of how the flavor takes me back to my childhood, or how my grandmother passed down her secret recipe. Truth is, most of the recipes in this cookbook are the iteration of several errors rather than glowing successes. My stories would be more along the lines of " . . . only after three attempts at this recipe did I realize that adding some water to the meat would make it much juicier", or "my kids were in tears the first time I made this – a clear indication that I needed to reduce the garlic content". Along these same lines, I also elected not to include photographs. Most cookbooks have elegant, award-worthy photos relevant to each recipe. While this certainly makes for great eye-candy, it can also involve significant costs related to either buying the photography equipment or hiring a professional. Because I wanted to keep this book affordable and also maintain its practical aspect, I bucked tradition and elected not to utilize food photography.

And away we go . . .

Now that you've been introduced to the cookbook, lets close with a discussion of its overall presentation. The next portion of the book covers a few concepts that will help you understand our relationship with sodium. We'll review some of the properties of sodium and outline how these properties make sodium a crucial component for our survival. We'll also look at why sodium is so prevalent within the food industry and discuss how sodium is involved in everything from flavor to preservation. Because you're likely here due to a desire to reduce your sodium intake, I'll then outline for you my own medical journey that led me to a low-sodium lifestyle and highlight why I intend to stay there. After that, we'll enter into the cookbook portion of this book. Because the Nutrition Facts label is intimately involved in the recipe format for this cookbook, we'll discuss the layout of the label and highlight its various components. We'll then take a look at the recipe layout for this book and also address some of the sodium-specific ingredients that I use in my recipes. Finally, we'll arrive at the recipe section, where you'll have a selection of 100 recipes covering breakfasts, sides, entrées, and desserts to help get (or keep) you on your low-sodium journey.

I hope you find that this isn't just another 'low-sodium cookbook' and that it provides you some valuable information about living a low-sodium lifestyle while also introducing you to some tasty recipes. What I share in this cookbook has been successful for me and I hope that the information I have learned along the way can be successful for you as well.

Understanding our relationship with sodium

To some it might seem a little strange how sodium gets as much attention as it does when it comes to food. After all, sodium is just one of many physical elements – along with carbon, potassium, and iron, among others – that our body requires in order to function properly. Still, we don't seem to hear as much about those other elements as we do sodium. Truth be told, sodium by itself shouldn't receive any additional attention given that it functions to fulfil a specific role in our metabolism just like those other elements. However, in this day and age when easily accessible food and drink allow us to supply excess sodium to our bodies, that excess intake can complicate normal physiological processes within our body which over time can manifest as health concerns. If we don't take corrective actions – such as reducing our sodium intake – those concerns can lead to significant health complications. To help you understand the complex relationship we have with sodium and how it can affect our health, this chapter is dedicated to providing an overview of what sodium is, how it interacts with our body, and why the characteristics of sodium cause it to be so prevalent within the food industry.

Sodium's Role in the Body

First, let's discuss some of sodium's basic principles. At its simplest, sodium is an element – the 6th most common element on the planet comprising nearly 3% of the earth's crust. Despite its prevalence, pure sodium is not normally found in nature; rather, it is typically combined with one or more additional elements to form what is known as a compound. You are probably quite familiar with many of these compounds which can include sodium chloride (i.e. table salt) or sodium bicarbonate (i.e. baking soda), among others. Because sodium is typically found in its compound form, our sodium intake is largely tied to consumption of one of these compounds.

When present in our body – sodium exists as an ion. This simply means that sodium is an atom with a particular electrical charge, and in the case of sodium that charge is "+" (i.e. 'positive'). Because of sodium's positive charge, our body operates in part by manipulating the movement of sodium ions in order to regulate two primary events: 1) facilitating nerve and muscle activity and 2) regulation of body fluid. Therefore, despite often unflattering reports about how sodium is responsible for a lot of negative health problems, sodium is indeed *required* by our body in order to function as designed. Next, we'll take a look at these processes in more detail in order to help understand why sodium is critical for normal body function.

Nerve and Muscle Signaling

You've probably heard at some point that your muscles move as a result of 'electricity'. In a way, that's certainly true. The 'electricity' component that you often hear about comes in part from your body's manipulation of sodium ions at the cellular level. Because your body is capable of manipulating sodium ions, and because those ions have a positive charge, your body is in effect controlling the flow of electricity.

Normally, sodium ions exist in a higher concentration outside of your cells. More specifically, they have a higher concentration in the area just outside of your cell membrane. In thinking back to the positive charge that is associated with sodium ions, a high concentration of those positive ions in the area outside of the cell membrane creates an overall positive charge in that area. Conversely, the interior cell – which holds a much lower concentration of sodium and other positively-charged ions – is considered as negatively charged relative to outside of the cell.

To generate a nerve signal that can activate your muscles, your body manipulates this overall positive charge. A response initiated within the brain causes sodium ions to rush across the cell membrane and into the cell interior (see Figure 1). This rush of sodium occurs due to the opening of 'gates' within sodium channels. Because only a

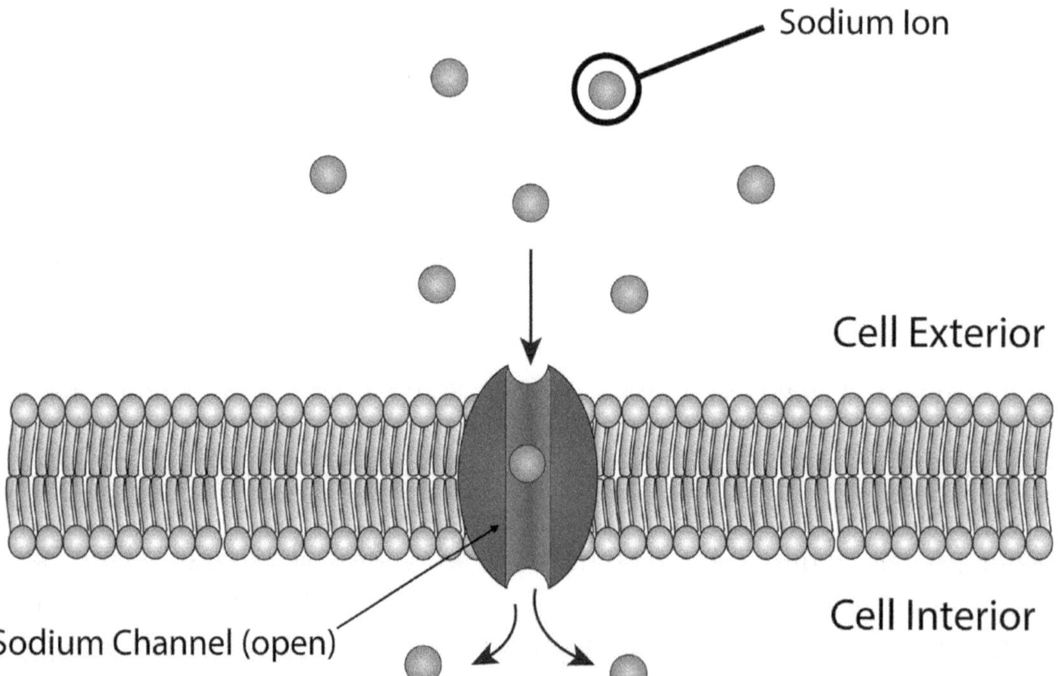

Figure 1. Sodium normally exists in a higher concentration outside of the cell. When the sodium channel opens, sodium is able to rush across the cell membrane (through the channel) and enter the cell interior, thus changing the charge inside the cell to 'positive'.

specific number of channels open and allow sodium to enter the cell, this inward rush of sodium occurs in a very small, prescribed section of the cell membrane. And in this small area where the sodium ions rush in, the interior of the cell becomes positively charged, thereby reversing the negative charge it had prior to the sodium ions rushing in.

So what does this change in one small area have to do with sending a nerve signal or activating a muscle? Well, as this change in the charge occurs in one very small area of the membrane, it triggers an identical change in charge in the area immediately next to the first, then the area next to that, and so on across the length of the cell membrane. This series of actions creates a 'wave' of positive charges that ultimately traverses the length of a nerve or muscle cell and is responsible for creating actions such as contraction of muscle. Why then do our nerves not 'fire' all the time, or our muscles not stay contracted constantly? The answer again relates back to sodium and our body's manipulation of the positive sodium ion. As soon as sodium ions rush into the cell and change the overall charge inside the cell to positive, our body immediately begins pumping those sodium ions back outside of the cell where they belong. Whereas sodium channels allow sodium ions to rush into the cell interior, sodium *pumps* serve to pump those same ions back to the area outside of the cell. When enough sodium ions have been pumped out, the cell interior is returned back to its original negative charge, thereby stopping all activity. So, just like how sodium enters the cell in an organized flow that travels across the length of the muscle or nerve cell, the removal of sodium from the cell interior also occurs in a similar fashion so as to cause the nerve transmission or muscle contraction to stop. Furthermore, this cycle of sodium entry and removal has to happen many times over milliseconds just to create one muscle contraction! It's actually a quite fascinating process as to how our body handles this intricate control of sodium so flawlessly.

To imagine what this whole series of cellular sodium manipulation looks like, think of throwing a rock into a pond. You see the ripples start from the area where the rock landed, and you see them flow out in all directions (See Figure 2). Think of the front of each ripple as the initial rush of sodium into the cell (and subsequent change in charge in one small area), followed by the back of each ripple which represents the pumping out of sodium and returning the cell back to its normal resting charge. This is then immediately followed by another cycle, and another, just like the repeated ripples on a pond. The actual breakdown of events are quite a bit more complicated (and teeming with biochemistry concepts that we don't need to cover), but imagining ripples spreading across a pond is an adequate representation of how sodium is manipulated to generate nerve signals and muscle contractions in your body.

Fluid Regulation

Besides its involvement in nerve and muscle cell signaling events, sodium is also intricately involved in regulating fluid levels within your body. As living organisms, we

Figure 2. Ripples extending out from a central source are a representation of how the body manipulates sodium in order to transmit nerve signals and generate muscle contraction.

require an intricate fluid balance within different areas of our body. On a macro-level, if fluid builds up too much in our body we may feel bloated or perhaps notice a degree of swelling. Should this swelling occur in certain areas of our body such as the brain, it could become fatal. Therefore, it is imperative that our body precisely regulate our fluid levels, and it does this through a variety of processes. For example, when our fluid levels become low our body simply stimulates us to drink by activating our thirst mechanism. Conversely, when fluid levels get too high, water is removed from the blood via the kidneys and accumulates as urine. But as mentioned, these processes are described at a macro-level. To understand how sodium is involved in fluid regulation we need to take a much more micro-level (i.e. 'cellular') approach.

Because sodium is a required component for normal physiologic function, our body doesn't simply get rid of any sodium that we might consume. In other words, our body views *normal* levels of sodium as essential for ensuring that we are able to function properly. Actually, normal body function is represented in part by the fact that our body is able to keep the sodium it needs while getting rid of the excess. In other words, a healthy body is healthy in part because it is able to maintain a proper sodium balance. When certain processes in our body are not working correctly, or in cases in which we continually feed sodium into our bodies at higher levels than what is needed, complications can start to occur. For example, if our kidneys are not functioning correctly, they may not be able to remove sodium from the bloodstream to the urine at a high enough rate. This in turn causes the sodium level in our body to become elevated. To further complicate things, healthy sodium concentrations are not equal across all areas of our body. For example, sodium in the blood must be maintained within a relatively tight window between 135-145 mEq/L (i.e. milliequivalents per liter). However, the sodium concentration inside of the cell is around 12mM (millimolar) while a concentration of 140mM must be maintained outside of the cell. If these specific ranges are not maintained, serious complications that can range from dehydration to death can occur.

To maintain sodium within the respective normal ranges, our body must work to balance out our sodium consumption practices. If our body detects that the sodium level is decreasing in any particular area (e.g. blood, outside of the cells, etc.), it will inhibit the processes such as urination that normally remove sodium from the bloodstream. Doing so will keep additional sodium within the bloodstream until acceptable sodium levels are reached. Conversely, when we consume excess sodium our body simply activates a series of processes that increases the elimination of sodium through the urine. For healthy individuals, excess sodium consumption isn't much of an issue since their body can easily handle the removal process. For other individuals, though, either their body does not function as required to remove excess sodium (likely due to a disease), or they continually consume such high sodium amounts that their body struggles to keep sodium levels within the required range. When these events occur, sodium begins to accumulate within the body. That in turn is the source of many sodium-related health issues that we face.

When sodium levels begin to accumulate, one of the first actions that the body will do is to retain fluid. The reason for this retention of fluid is quite simple. In response to the rising sodium levels, our body attempts to dilute the sodium concentration by simply retaining more fluid – in turn creating a greater fluid volume within the body. While your body creates this fluid retention as a sort of protective mechanism to maintain an adequate sodium concentration, the excess fluid can cause health-related issues such as high blood pressure due to the strain on the heart required to pump the extra fluid around the body. For people like me with inner ear issues, the excess fluid can cause problems within the highly sensitive vestibular system.

It's about balance, not *elimination*

When it comes to sodium and our body, it must be reiterated that sodium is *required* by our body to function normally. So much of what we hear from friends and on the news about needing to lower our sodium intake is often true, but it shouldn't be misinterpreted to mean 'the lower, the better'. In fact, too low of a sodium intake can ultimately be fatal as well. The *required* minimal sodium intake differs somewhat across experts, with some saying as little as 500mg/day is adequate while others recommend an intake level of 1000mg/day or more. This value is somewhat dependent upon an individual's activity level. For example, sodium is a component of sweat, so increased perspiration causes a greater amount of sodium to be removed from the body. Therefore, individuals who engage in sweaty activity should likely consume a higher level of sodium in order to account for any sodium being lost through sweat.

When engaging in a low-sodium lifestyle, I can't stress enough that your goal is never *no-sodium*. Trying to drastically eliminate sodium from one's diet can contribute to multiple negative health conditions as well as a potentially life-threatening condition known as hyponatremia. Therefore, always strive to keep a healthy level of sodium in your diet even when actively trying to stay low-sodium, and never aim for a complete elimination of sodium as it is unhealthy and potentially dangerous.

In terms of the sodium intake *recommended* daily for most healthy adults in the U.S., the FDA uses a value of 2,300mg, or the equivalent of about one teaspoon of table salt. In actuality, though, the average American consumes around 3,400mg of sodium per day – much higher than the recommended level and likely contributing to many of the sodium-related health conditions that occur. It's important to note that this recommended intake of 2,300mg/day has been established for *healthy* individuals – there is no established intake level for those of us on a low-sodium diet. Recommendations are often set by medical providers and based on the individual's particular situation but typically range from 1,000-2,000mg per day. My own personal intake preference as a vestibular patient is around 1,000-1,200mg of sodium per day as I have found that level to be effective at keeping my Ménière's symptoms suppressed. Interestingly, Ménière's disease research suggests that it's not necessarily the amount of sodium that we consume but instead may be linked to sudden *fluctuations* in the level of sodium within our body. Such fluctuations could include a sharp rise in blood sodium levels after consuming a high-sodium meal; therefore, maintaining a consistent blood sodium level appear to be beneficial. Since maintaining a low-sodium diet I have found that staying in the 1,000-1,200mg per day range has kept my symptoms at bay. You may find a different range that works for you. The goal is always improved health, so keep trying until you find what works for you.

Sodium and the Food Industry

Now that you hopefully have a better understanding of sodium's role within our body, let's next look at the relationship between sodium and our food. Sodium seems to be in almost everything we eat, or as some people have told me, the things we really *want* to eat. I can understand where that statement comes from, as we often hear that sodium (or more specifically, 'salt') makes food taste better. Still, I have often questioned how much of our relationship with salt and food comes from habit rather than a true need or desire. In other words, do we add salt at the dinner table because the salt is sitting there (likely), or do we actually detect an inadequate flavor issue and add precisely enough salt to develop that perfect flavor we are seeking (not likely). That may be a question for which we'll never truly know the answer, but I have to admit that I used to be quite guilty of the former myself.

Regardless of why we add salt, it's undeniable that salt – and sodium – are intricately involved with the foods we eat. While adding salt at the dinner table does play a role in contributing to our overall sodium intake, it's also important to recognize the food industry's involvement with salt and sodium. Therefore, we'll next examine sodium's role in the food industry and how it impacts many of the foods we eat. By understanding sodium's involvement in our food, it can allow us to make better decisions about our food and thereby improve our sodium consumption habits.

When it comes to the food industry, sodium – in its salt form – has three major aspects that influence its involvement in our food: flavor enhancement, preservation, and chemical reactions. The first of these three – flavor enhancement – is well-known as to how salt can improve or contribute flavor to a variety of foods. We won't spend any time discussing the physiology of taste buds or how flavor works, though, as all we need to know as low-sodium consumers is that the food industry recognizes that salt can improve food flavor and therefore salt is often added as a flavor-enhancement tool. If you have any doubts about how salt can affect flavor, try to eat a poorly brined pickle – you'll quickly recognize that salt has as much importance in creating the classic pickle taste as sugar does in transforming unsweetened chocolate into a delectable treat.

In addition to flavor enhancement, salt is commonly used as a preservative by the food industry. Science has revealed that several factors can be involved in a food's shelf life such as exposure to oxygen or elevated temperatures as well as infiltration by bacteria or mold. Therefore, salt is often added as an ingredient in many food types such as canned foods that are susceptible to spoilage, as the addition of salt is effective at prolonging shelf life. Without the addition of salt to the food or container, microbes such as bacteria could thrive unimpeded in the dark and moist environment. The addition of salt during the canning process ensures that the microbes cannot survive the high-sodium environment. Interestingly, even if a particular salt concentration doesn't kill the microbes, it keeps them so busy trying to get the sodium out of their microbe bodies that they cannot effectively reproduce. Therefore, in cases where a salty environment may not kill the microbes, it can be effective at keeping them from multiplying.

Even with the knowledge we have specific to sodium's potential negative effects on our health, don't expect much change by the food industry in terms of halting its use of salt as a preservative. The effectiveness of salt in extending shelf life, coupled with its low cost, make it an outstanding preservative in terms of cost-to-benefit ratio. Other preservation techniques such as chilling or freezing have been used, but relative to cost and effectiveness, salt and its inherent sodium composition continues to have overwhelming support. Still, many manufacturers are recognizing the demand for lower-sodium products, and a surge in the number of 'reduced sodium' or 'no salt added' products has been noticeable in recent years. For those of us on a low-sodium diet it is certainly hoped that this trend continues to grow, and it is encouraging that we have a wealth of lower-sodium products available to us now which we did not have even a decade ago.

Along with having roles in flavor enhancement and food preservation, sodium is also intimately involved in the production of some foods. This involvement is often seen in baked goods such as cakes where ingredients like baking soda or its relative, baking powder, are used. While we are all familiar with these products, the methods by which these sodium-based ingredients can influence food production may not be as familiar. Baking soda is comprised of *sodium bicarbonate* while baking powder is made up of *sodium bicarbonate* plus *cream of tartar* (and sometimes corn starch). It's the chemical makeup of these components that makes them so beneficial in food preparation. Baking soda, when in the presence of an acidic (i.e. pH of less than 7.0) ingredient such as lemon juice or buttermilk, reacts to cause a production of gas that creates tiny pockets within the dough or cake mix that we are all familiar with. Baking powder, on the other hand, does not require an acid in the ingredients. The included cream of tartar supplied in baking powder provides the acidic component needed to create the necessary chemical reaction. Therefore, almost any liquid (e.g. water, milk, etc.) used in a recipe is capable of triggering the production of gas that is essential for the development of items such as baked quick breads and cakes.

For baked goods involving yeast, baking soda and baking powder are not typically included in the recipe as the yeast is used to create the small pockets within the dough. However, sodium is often still present in significantly high amounts in yeast-based items such as breads. In fact, the staple ingredients of many bread dough recipes are flour, water, yeast, and salt, whereby salt has multiple roles related to the development of the dough. For example, salt can inhibit the activity of yeast. This results in a slower rise of the dough and can generate a stronger overall dough since gas pockets – formed by the release of carbon dioxide from the yeast – may not grow as large in the presence of salt-infused dough. Salt can also serve to provide strength to gluten within the dough, thereby allowing the dough to better contain these pockets of gas formed by the carbon dioxide.

Despite the importance of salt within yeast-based bread recipes, there are modifications that can be made in order to reduce the sodium content. For example, reducing the recipe's salt content by half or utilizing potassium chloride (i.e. salt substitute) in place of salt have been recommended, but doing so may cause noticeable differences in the structural integrity of the dough which may in turn require multiple recipe adjustments in order to get it to the expected final product.

Conclusion

We've covered a lot of material in a short time in this chapter, but it was my intent to provide you some key information that would allow you to have a better understanding of sodium in order to help you navigate the low-sodium lifestyle. Remember first and foremost that our bodies *require* sodium to function, so it should never be your intent to eliminate sodium from your diet. Also, remember that sodium plays vital roles in the food industry. Improved shelf life as well as structural integrity of certain food items are influenced by salt and therefore will likely have a significant sodium content. Because of sodium's prevalence in our food, it is important that we constantly monitor the sodium content of food products we consume. If you would like more information on what we covered in this chapter, I recommend that you check out my book *Living Low-Sodium* where we take a much more in-depth look at several of these aspects of sodium.

In the next chapter I'll take you on a brief trip through my own sodium journey so that you can understand my passion for living a low-sodium lifestyle and why I felt it important to write this cookbook. It's been a long journey for me to get where I am in terms of my own involvement with sodium, and like your own personalized story you'll find that I certainly have my reasons for switching to a low-sodium diet – and staying there.

My low sodium journey

As I mentioned early on, people take on a low-sodium lifestyle for various reasons. Some individuals may have read about the negative impact that excess sodium can have on their health and so they choose to adopt dietary measures to reduce their sodium intake. Others may have been diagnosed with a medical condition – or are on a path toward eventually being diagnosed – and need to reduce their sodium intake in order to diminish the effects of their medical condition. For me, I found out in 2011 that I fall into the latter group when I was diagnosed with a condition called Ménière's disease. For several years I had been suffering from a variety of strange symptoms including headaches, stuffiness in my right ear, constant imbalance and dizziness, jumpy vision, and sudden attacks of severe vertigo, nausea, and vomiting. In a period of just a few months I regressed from an energetic, athletic individual to someone who had difficulty walking down long hallways and exhibited near-constant anxiety.

It was only after several years of symptoms and visits to many different medical practitioners that I was finally able to find a physician who accurately diagnosed me. My anger after having been told during prior medical visits to 'just relax' or to just get more sleep was finally validated after receiving a definitive diagnosis. At first there was a bit of frustration and even confusion given that I had not even the faintest understanding of what Ménière's was, thereby leaving me with a debilitating medical condition that I knew nothing about. And as I grew to understand over the following weeks, it became more clear that the medical literature knew little about Ménière's as well given that the cause was not understood, a rationale to explain the debilitating symptoms was not known, and a cure did not exist. What I did learn was that Ménière's was a condition affecting the inner ear, possibly related to fluid levels, and it was not fatal. So while there was no cure for this debilitating condition I now had, it was also clear that I would not die – even though during the attacks I certainly felt as though I wanted to die. In simpler terms, I was likely stuck feeling like this for the rest of my life.

My initial treatment for Ménière's consisted of a regimen of medicines designed to increase urination (i.e. 'diuretics') along with betahistine to increase blood flow to my inner ear. I was also instructed to reduce both my sodium intake and my caffeine consumption. This information was a bit ironic given that about two decades earlier I clearly remember joking with a friend that the only time I planned to disobey my doctor would be when he or she told me I had to give up caffeine or salt. But back then I was a naïve college kid, not the panicked, unsteady shred of my former self that now existed. If this treatment plan of medication and sodium reduction did not work, the next step would involve steroid injections delivered through my eardrum. That was not a direction I was wanting to go, but still, the attacks were so severe that I would do anything to make them stop. So I listened to the medical advice and wholeheartedly quit drinking coffee and quit salting my food. In my mind, I was reducing my sodium intake as required.

Giving up these longtime staples in my diet was surprisingly easy. I went from 10-15 cups of coffee over the course of a morning down to zero. There was no tapering, no withdrawals. And it paid off. Certain strange tics that I had been experiencing went away. When I stopped adding the ample amounts of salt to my food, I noticed that my vision was no longer jumpy, and the ear that had felt stuffy for several years now seemed to have its normal hearing range back. Could this really be working? Along with the prescribed medicines, this dietary switch seemed to be doing the job. All this despite the fact that I was only avoiding caffeine and salty foods and not adding salt at the table. However, I was still oblivious to the sodium already in many foods. Things got so good that a few months into the process I quit taking both medications – a boost to my ego and to our bank account given that one of them was not covered by insurance. For several months I kept feeling better. So much better that I largely forgot about my medical issues. Unfortunately, forgetfulness is a bad thing, as it can lead to complacency.

And that is just what occurred. About six months after making my sodium and caffeine switch, my world came crashing down in May of 2012. I had been feeling great for months, and the birth of my first child was just two weeks away. Without a care in the world I put a roast in the crock pot, along with two packets of onion soup mix. I consumed the roast with the same enthusiasm anyone would expect from a red-blooded American male who has a pile of juicy meat and broth placed in front of him. It was delicious, and I probably ate much more than I should have. In the following days I had no concerns at all. Then, the first warning shot was fired. Upon approaching a stoplight, I had an immense 'whooshing' sensation like what I had experienced during my worst Ménière's days. I nervously drove the rest of the way home with no incident. Then nothing more occurred that night. But the next day, while stepping off a curb to cross a busy street for lunch, a rapid and major vertigo attack hit and I collapsed to the ground – right in the middle of an intersection. People were rushing over to me as I laid on the ground feeling around with my hands in order to determine my body position. Within about 30 seconds the symptoms abated briefly, giving me just enough time to get somewhere safe before the worst part of the attack began. And just 15 minutes later, it started. I had the worst vertigo, vomiting, and nausea attack of all my years with the illness.

Despite the despair brought about by thoughts that my Ménière's had returned unprompted, I soon realized that the onion soup mix was likely to blame. I had to accept the fact that my own complacency about staying low-sodium had invited my Ménière's back with a vengeance. The next day I was lucky enough to get an appointment with my ear doctor. I sat on the paper-lined examination table and bawled like a 3-year-old. I was convinced that my Ménière's was back, worsened by the fact that I had finally started to boldly believe that I had conquered it. Through my slobbery, runny-nosed attempts to talk I explained to the physician my frustrations about how I hadn't been salting my food, and that I had been eating salads – which "don't have any salt" according to my own belief at the time. I still remember the next thing he said, for strangely enough it was what I consider to be the re-boot of my low-sodium journey. "Well, the salad dressing does". Those five words struck a chord with me. It jolted me enough to get me to stop bawling. My mind raced as I remembered how I would slather a large salad with half a bottle of salad dressing, unknowingly soaking the salad with sodium. The following five minutes were spent in directed conversation about how it's not 'salt', *per se*, but sodium that I need to monitor. We talked at length about how sodium is hidden in many of our everyday food items, like salad dressing or fast food. Or . . . onion soup mix.

If I've ever had an epiphany in my life, that would be the day. I went home and started looking at food labels. I mean I *really* started looking at them. I quickly recognized how much sodium I was actually consuming during the day. Even though I had largely been feeling better, I was likely never going to feel as good as I *could* feel since I was still consuming an excessive amount of sodium – despite the fact that I wasn't salting my food. It quickly became apparent to me that 'healthy food' does not necessarily translate to 'low-sodium' food. In other words, my plan of using canned, diced tomatoes might seem viable for creating a healthier pasta sauce than using sauce from a jar, but those canned tomatoes were still causing me to consume a lot of sodium given the quantity of food that I was eating.

Every new fact I learned about sodium and food became a mini realization as I could almost always relate some small aspect back to my own eating habits. Over time I learned more about sodium, such as how it affects our physiology and is required for our overall health. It was a rush, of sorts, to absorb all this information as I knew that every tidbit would contribute to an improvement in my symptoms. Meanwhile, I kept getting healthier. The dizziness had stopped. The headaches were gone. No vertigo attacks had occurred in months. I was actually feeling normal again. Somehow I was beating a disease that had no cure. And this time around I would not allow myself to get complacent; rather, I would charge forward with this newfound lifestyle.

Though I was never much of a runner prior to the onset of my Ménière's, I now saw running – or more specifically, perspiration – as a way to remove additional sodium from my body. Eventually, I entered a half marathon. Then a marathon. Then a half-Ironman, followed a year later by a full Ironman. And then another. All while countering medical research that says sodium intake should be increased in order to maintain one's health when exercising in hot, humid climates. In the span of a few years I had gone from having difficulty maintaining my balance to finishing Ironman races and living relatively symptom-free. And soon I will be able to say that I've been able to maintain this balance between health, sodium intake, and physical activity for over a decade. Rarely, a negative thought will creep in as to whether staying low-sodium will cease to stave off my Ménière's symptoms, but those negative thoughts are short-lived and I never dwell on them. I'm having too much fun attending my daughters' sporting events, exercising, and participating in our family's great life to worry about them.

While I can say that I feel largely 'normal' these days, I am certain that the reason that I feel this way is because I maintain my low-sodium diet. Therefore, it could reasonably be stated that my current good health is intimately tied to the food I eat. Looking through my pantry and refrigerator reveals that 100% of the personal food decisions I make are based on sodium content. For example, I only buy meat that has not been injected with brine or seasonings. All my spices are sodium-free. The salsa I use has the lowest sodium content (95mg per tablespoon) of all the brands in the local stores. At time I feel like my life with food has become like Cypher in the original Matrix movie, where he is staring at a screen full of computer code but tells Neo that all he sees is "blonde, brunette, redhead". Similarly, instead of food preferences in the grocery aisle, all I now see are sodium levels – "too high", "OK to buy", "find the low-sodium version", and so on, and so on. While this may sound tedious or even weird to some, because my Ménière's attacks were so debilitating and so terrifying, not one part of me misses the taste of foods that I know are high in sodium. To me, the risk just isn't worth it. We do still have a few packaged foods and snacks in my pantry that have excessively-high sodium levels, but those are for my wife and kids. I don't want to force them into my low-sodium lifestyle as I know that they have no real reason to participate. But for the most part, they've been on this journey alongside me without any complaints. And I love the fact that they don't *have* to join me.

As a married man with kids who had to learn to cook low-sodium, I can't help but think of some of what my family has been put through in having to eat some of my early attempts at recipes. Even though I like to cook, I also enjoy the peace-of-mind that cooking my own food brings since I don't have to worry about whether some excess-sodium ingredient has made its way into the food. Taking on a new style of cooking in the early years after my switch to low-sodium certainly resulted in a lot of failures when it comes to recipes – and my family suffered the brunt of those failures. But the process of creating and reworking recipes also opened up a few major successes and eventually created quite a few great meals along the way. And what really made the difference for me in cooking my own recipes stemmed from the *amount* of food that I consume compared to what I would often find in normal 'low sodium' recipes.

In recognizing that I eat more food than the average person, I started working on developing recipes early on that would provide enough food not only for me but also my family of four. And as I went further down the rabbit hole that reveals how sodium is used in the food industry, I learned that I wasn't limited to beef or pasta dishes. With some selective shopping practices I could still enjoy certain bacon and pork items, for example, which led to a whole new category of recipes. Then, thanks to a Christmas gift from my wife, sodium-free chicken and beef stock entered the equation. In a flash, soups, stews, and many other dishes were on the menu. Slowly I was finding out that low-sodium cooking didn't mean limited food options. With a little effort up front, it was becoming damn-near limitless.

After a decade of tinkering, modifying, and finalizing a series of recipes that we enjoy as a family, I decided that it was time to consolidate them into a cookbook. And that's where we have arrived. This cookbook is my own collection of recipes that I make for my family. Truth be told, I have probably tried converting over 250 recipes to a low-sodium format. And if I put in the effort, there are probably thousands more recipes that are awaiting their low-sodium modification.

So many times I have seen recipes that include a teaspoon of salt in the ingredient list for, say, an entire casserole. In my experience, there is just no significant improvement in taste by adding that amount of salt for such a large dish. Or, I'll see recipes that state 'season the chicken with salt and pepper' but then prepare that seasoned chicken in a skillet full of simmering chicken broth. Again, to me the addition of salt in such a case isn't warranted as it doesn't contribute to the taste of the recipe and only serves to add several hundred milligrams of sodium. Perhaps I could have taken those type of recipes and replaced salt with a sodium-free salt substitute like potassium chloride. But that wouldn't have fit my intent for this cookbook, as I wanted to assemble a collection of recipes that I feel work fine *without* the addition of salt (or salt substitute). Those are the recipes that I've utilized and have been able to modify in order to still get ample flavor but without the addition of unnecessary sodium.

Now that you know my story and understand my own reasons for being low sodium, it's time to get into the recipes. First, though, we'll take a semi-detour and spend some time in the next chapter discussing the layout of the recipes in this book so that you have an understanding of what the information represents on each recipe page. We'll also take some time to discuss the Nutrition Facts label, that important information source found on the back of almost all food packages which I treat as my own low sodium guide. All of the recipes in this book include a Nutrition Facts label, and it's important that you have a clear understanding of how to interpret the Nutrition Facts label in order to understand the nutritional – and sodium – information for each recipe.

How to use this recipe book

What is a cookbook without recipes, right? As I stated early on, one of my primary goals for this cookbook is to help you better understand our relationship with sodium – particularly how it interacts with our body and why it's so prevalent in our food. Now that you have a foundational knowledge of sodium, let's turn our attention toward the recipes! Before we do, though, we need to spend a little bit of time outlining this book's general recipe layout so that you are oriented to the structure of each recipe and how they are formatted.

For starters, I think it's important to point out now that I am not a chef – I am a cook. And for the past near decade I have been a low-sodium cook. My only formal cooking experience occurred while working at a small-town restaurant while in high school 30 years ago and a brief two-month stint at a fast-food restaurant chain in 8th grade. My point in saying this is because I don't follow a lot of the traditional cooking rules. In fact, classically trained chefs would likely cringe repeatedly if watching me prepare a meal. But I've never really been about developing exquisite recipes; rather, my interest has been in two main areas: practicality and sodium content. Therefore, you won't find instructions such as *salt the water before adding the uncooked pasta*. I know many cookbooks and websites report that it's essential to salt the water, but I personally don't feel that it makes a noticeable difference and instead only contributes additional sodium.

In another break from tradition, when browning my ground beef I often include any diced raw vegetables (e.g. onion, carrots, bell pepper, etc.) that need to cook. In my experience, browning the ground beef and then cooking the vegetables separately in olive oil creates an unnecessary time expense. Therefore, to save time I will often combine the two steps. Similarly, you won't find many uses of fresh herbs or spices in my book nor will you find ingredients like 'fresh squeezed lemon juice'. While I know that many outstanding cooks and chefs prefer the fresh versions, my goal of providing ample amounts of good-tasting food is achievable through an array of dried herb and spice options as well as bottled lemon or lime juice. Any minimally detectable sacrifice I might be making in flavor is easily offset by cost savings, shelf life, and convenience. You are of course welcome to introduce your own cooking preferences!

The next thing to keep in mind when using this book is that while it is indeed a cookbook, its concept is designed around 'big eaters'. Therefore most of the recipes – with the exclusion of a few sides – have a relatively large quantity of food. Consequently, you won't find many recipes that qualify as low-calorie, low-carb, or low-cholesterol (though a few do, as outlined in the Appendix). If you don't partake in large portion sizes yourself, you might want to halve the ingredient quantities or have a plan to freeze what may be an ample amount of leftovers.

Recipe Layout

For the most part, the recipes in this book follow the same general format found in all standard cookbooks in that there is a structured ingredient list along with instructions on how to prepare the meal. As I mentioned early in this book, my recipes are succinct and to-the-point. Therefore, there are no step-by-step narratives nor ancillary discussions such as how long the prepared recipe will last while frozen. Instead, I elected to provide you with the basic information necessary to prepare each recipe. Next, I'll outline the various sections used for each recipe in this book.

Prep and Cook times

Near the top of each recipe you will find the estimated preparation ("prep") time and cooking time required to prepare the recipe. Understand that these are quite arbitrary and are based upon what it takes me to prepare the meal. As a multitasker, I often have several tasks going at once with the intent of having them all completed on schedule so that the recipe preparation runs smoothly. Not everyone cooks this way, so I have tried to estimate the required time to account for all cooking styles. For example, because I've literally made the *Spaghetti with Meat Sauce* recipe at least 100 times (due to my kids' repeated requests), the overlapping of steps has allowed me to prepare the entire recipe in approximately 15 minutes from start to finish. This is quite an unrealistic time for most cooks, so I have adjusted the times based upon what I think most people will require. The prep and cook times aren't perfect, but they should give you an adequate representation of what to expect for each recipe.

Recipe Quantity Indicators

Next you will find an area titled "Recipe Quantity" along with a small graphic that represents a sort of meter. This section of each recipe is intended to visually represent how much food the recipe will provide. As I mentioned earlier, I elected to not use serving or portion sizes for this cookbook given that big eaters like me don't typically adhere to any portion sizes. I instead chose to use these 'recipe quantity' indicators to represent four general classifications of how much food each recipe will provide. Like the 'prep' and 'cook' times listed above, however, these recipe quantity indicators are quite arbitrary in nature as they are developed from my own opinion. To outline what they represent, I have included below an overview of the range of recipe quantity indicators:

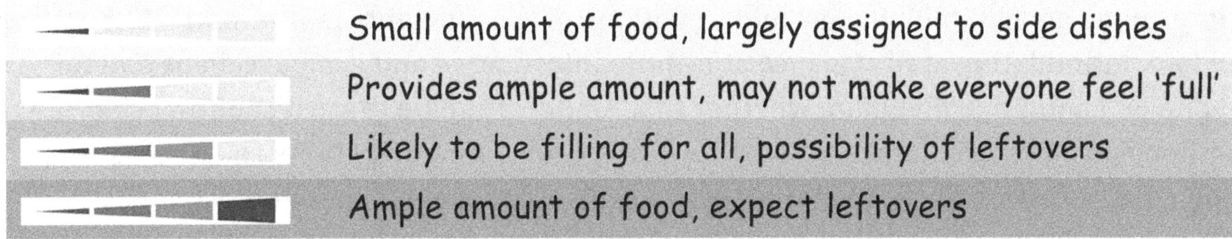

Nutrition Facts Label

Instead of a list of nutritional information at the bottom of the page as is commonly used in many cookbooks, the nutritional information for my recipes is detailed using the format of the Food and Drug Administration's (FDA) 'Nutrition Facts label', identical to what can be found on the back of most food packages. The Nutrition Facts label is what many of us on a low-sodium diet use to guide our food purchases as it clearly and precisely outlines the sodium content of a particular food item. Given our familiarity with the Nutrition Facts label, I felt that it would fit perfectly in a cookbook that emphasizes low-sodium recipes. Because of the information that the Nutrition Facts label provides, we'll next discuss the sections of the label in order to help you understand what it represents and how you can use it to plan out your sodium intake.

In looking at the standard Nutrition Facts panel (see Figure 3), it's important to note that the current label has gone through many changes over the years with the intent

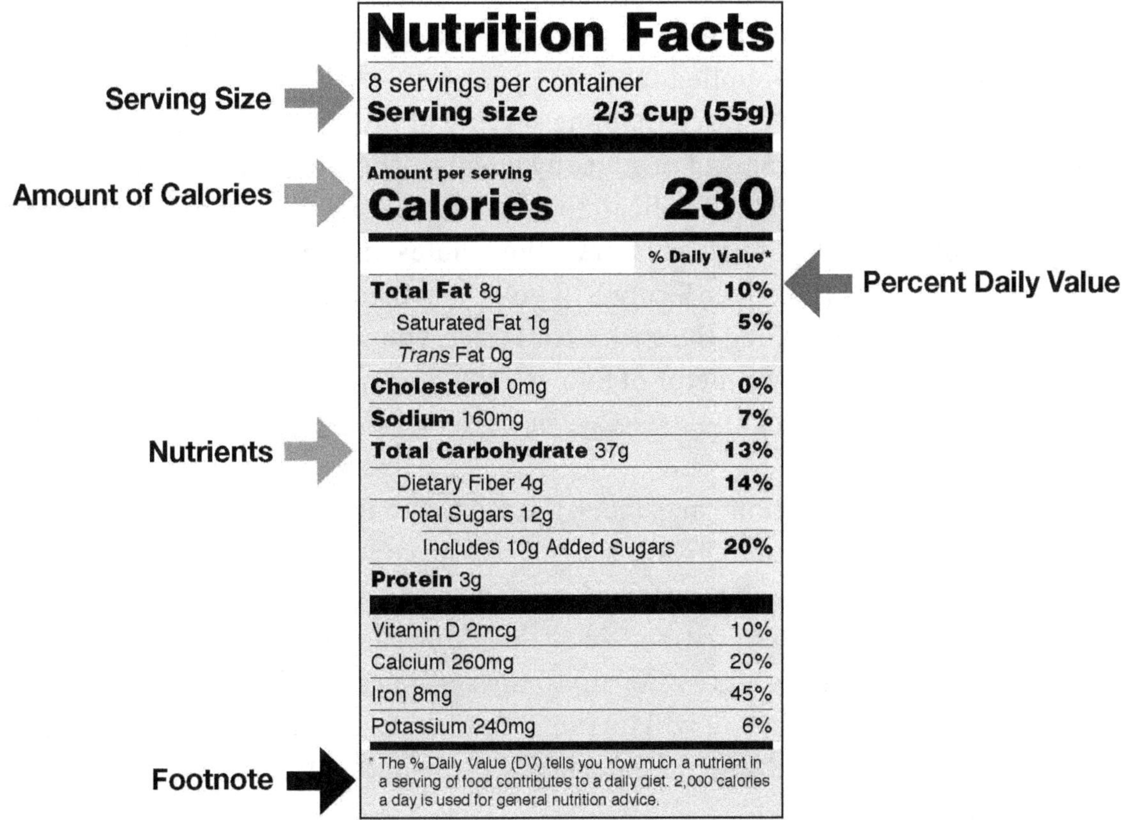

Figure 3. The standard Nutrition Facts label (shading added to represent individual sections)

of improving and simplifying our understanding of the nutrients in our food. While it may still look intimidating at first glance, it is quite informative and is an excellent tool for anyone on a modified diet plan, whether that modification be toward counting calories, monitoring cholesterol intake, or staying low-sodium. And despite its relatively simple design, the Nutrition Facts label is actually regulated through pages and pages of government documents outlining quantities, measurement units, and even font size. While there are significant requirements that food manufacturers have to meet in order to place the Nutrition Facts on a food package, the underlying intent is to protect and inform you the consumer.

At the top of the Nutrition Facts label is an area that is perhaps the most important part – *Serving Size.* Here you'll find two important components: serving size and servings per container. The reason for the importance is because *everything* on the Nutrition Facts label relates back to the individual serving size. So while you may have eaten a relatively small bag of snack food, that bag may have contained two or more actual servings despite the fact that there wasn't much more than a handful of food in the bag. Serving size is the 'amount customarily consumed' by an individual and was originally established using consumer surveys conducted decades ago by the FDA. While not always realistic for many of us, these serving sizes are recognized by the government and are the standard measurement used. So, while you may easily consume two cups of green beans in a sitting, the FDA maintains that ½ cup of green beans is the established serving size. If you do normally consume more than the serving size it doesn't mean that you are doing anything wrong or eating too much! Rather, the serving size simply specifies a reference amount that all included nutrients can be applied towards.

In looking at Figure 3, you can see that one serving of this product equals 2/3 of a cup as measured by size, or 55 grams of product by weight. Therefore, *all* nutritional information outlined on this label is specific to that 2/3 cup. You will also note that there are 8 servings per container. So, if you consumed the whole container's-worth of food, you would have eaten 8 servings (just over 5 cups). If you then needed to know how much sodium you consumed after finishing the entire container, you would need to multiply the listed sodium content (160mg) by a factor of 8 to get 1,280mg of sodium. Serving sizes come in all shapes, sizes, and amounts, so always be sure to check the serving size for all food products.

In moving down the Nutrition Facts label, the next item is the *Amount of Calories* section. For individuals interested in losing weight, calorie content is quite important and probably explains why the FDA took the step of increasing the font size of the calorie line for the most recent version of the Nutrition Facts label. Once again, the calories listed on the Nutrition Facts label in Figure 3 are relevant to the serving size. Therefore, if you consume 2/3 cup of the food item, you will intake 230 calories, but if you consume more than 2/3 cup you will need to multiply the calories by the representative number of servings that you ate.

Next up on the Nutrition Facts label is the *Nutrients* section. This portion of the label outlines the food product's fat, carbohydrate, and protein composition per serving along with a couple of specific nutrients (sodium and cholesterol) that are often of health-related interest in one's diet. Underneath the main Nutrient section of the label you will find a few additional vitamins and minerals including Vitamin D, Calcium, Iron, and Potassium.

To the right of the Nutrition area you will see a column of percentages under the heading of "% Daily Value". These percentages represent how much of the recommended daily amount of each nutrient is provided by this food item per serving – based on someone who intends to consume 2,000 calories per day. In the example label, eating 2/3 cup of the food product provides 7% of the sodium intake *recommended* for a healthy person on a 2,000 calorie-per-day diet. If, however, you ate 2 cups of the food item (i.e. three servings), you would then have consumed 21% of the total sodium recommended for a 2,000 calorie diet. For those of us on a low-sodium diet, you probably aren't aiming for the sodium intake level consistent with a healthy person on a 2,000 calorie diet and instead will be looking to achieve a lower intake. This highlights the notion that the Nutrition Facts label does not outline 'requirements' but rather 'recommendations'.

In this book I have elected to use most aspects of the Nutrition Facts panel. I say 'most' because I did not include the serving size nor the number of servings per container. This is because all Nutrition Facts labels for the recipes in this book represent the nutrition information for the entire dish rather than one serving. In other words, the complete recipe is equivalent to one serving on the respective Nutrition Facts label. Therefore, be aware that the % Daily Values will be somewhat high for most recipes in this book since they reflect the entire dish rather than a customary serving size.

It should also be pointed out how the nutritional information was determined for each recipe in this cookbook. There are multiple ways to arrive at a particular food product or recipe's Nutritional Facts. One way is to send the prepared food off to an analytical lab which chemically analyzes the food to determine its nutritional makeup. This method is customized to the actual food item itself yet incurs a significant expense that can run into the thousands of dollars. The second method for establishing a recipe's nutritional value is to sum up the reported values from each ingredient, relative to the amount of ingredient used. This 'summation' method is what was used to determine the nutrient information for each recipe in this cookbook.

A note about *Added Sugars*

Under the Carbohydrates section of the Nutrition Facts label is a line that states *Includes "X"g of Added Sugars.* This line can cause a little bit of confusion so I think it's important to address it in order to help you better understand what you are consuming. Added sugars are considered by the FDA to be any sugar *added* during the processing of a food item. This does not include naturally-occurring sugars such as found in many foods like fruits. Therefore, a food product listing 11 grams of sugar with 5 grams of added sugar means that 6 grams of naturally-occurring sugar was already in the food item.

The confusion comes in that single-ingredient items such as granulated sugar or honey do not have any 'added sugar' despite the fact that each is largely a sugar product itself. In other words, while each is largely comprised of sugar, no sugars are added during their manufacturing. As such, their Nutrition Facts label does not list an added sugar amount. However, any food which adds these items will list that amount as an 'added sugar'.

Whereas each recipe's Nutrition Facts label in this cookbook was built from individual ingredient Nutrition Facts quantities, the amount of added sugar can vary by recipe. Only those recipes which have ingredients listing an added sugar amount on their respective Nutrition Facts labels will be reflected on the recipe's Nutrition Facts label. Therefore, while sugar may be listed as an ingredient, because sugar does not have any added sugar, the recipe's Nutrition Facts label would not show an added sugar. Conversely, if an ingredient included an added sugar on its Nutrition Facts label, that added sugar would be accounted for in the recipe's final Nutrition Facts label.

Ingredient List

Now that we have outlined the basic layout of the recipe, let's start to look at some concepts related to ingredients that I use. Understanding my ingredient list is important, as the total sodium content of each recipe is inherent to the sodium makeup of the particular ingredients that I use. For example, adding a can of regular diced tomatoes in a recipe that calls for no-salt-added diced tomatoes can result in a final sodium value of 600mg or more (per can) higher than what is outlined on the recipe's Nutrition Facts label. Because of the importance of ingredients, I'll next go through some of the major ingredient categories to identify important aspects that I used in preparation of my recipes.

Meats:

I'm a certified meat eater, and the recipes in this cookbook reflect that characteristic. But to a low-sodium consumer, *caveat emptor* when it comes to meat products. I've learned over the years that even per category (beef, chicken, pork, and fish) the sodium content of these products can fluctuate tremendously. Let's discuss this in more detail:

- When selecting your meats, look for 'uninjected', or 'unbrined' meats. Many meat products are injected with a sodium solution designed to increase the size of the meat (also known as 'plumping') and/or improve flavor. Injected meats can have 10 times (or more) sodium than natural meat products. All recipes in this book use plain (non-seasoned) meat that has not been injected with brine. Look for meats on Styrofoam trays and wrapped in cellophane as well as tubes of ground beef when possible, but always double-check the Nutrition Facts label to be certain.

- When cooking, especially on thicker recipe items like meatloaf or Swiss steak, it is best practice to ensure that your meats have been thoroughly cooked through. The U.S. Department of Agriculture recommends an internal temperature of at least 165°F for poultry and ground meat, or 145°F for roast, steak, or pork chop products.

- Many of my recipes call for ground beef. There are a lot of options when it comes to the ratio of lean meat to fat, and my personal preference is ground chuck, the term used for meat with an 80:20 or 85:15 ratio of lean meat to fat. All ground beef nutrition information used in my recipes is derived from an 80:20 mix of ground chuck. Some will say that different recipes (e.g. meatloaf versus burger patties) call for specific ratios of fat to meat, but feel free to choose whatever ratio you prefer.

Canned vegetables:

- Whether it's diced tomatoes, black beans, green beans, or corn, most canned vegetables come with a healthy dose of sodium used as a preservative. Thankfully, in this day and age we have lower-sodium options with no real sacrifice in taste. Therefore, recipes in this cookbook use no-salt-added (NSA) canned vegetables. These products are not sodium-free but are packaged without a brine solution commonly used in the canning process. You can find the no-salt-added version for most canned vegetables and tomato products right alongside the regular version. If the no-salt-added version is not an option for you, most frozen vegetables are packaged with little to no sodium and can serve as a viable substitute. Still, be sure to check the Nutrition Facts label as some frozen products do receive a salt bath prior to freezing.

- You'll likely find quite a few options when it comes to different versions of canned vegetables. Even within no-salt-added versions you can still run into 'green beans' versus 'French-style green beans' and 'whole-kernel corn' versus 'sweet corn'. Use whichever canned style you prefer.

Herbs (and Spices):

- Almost all herbs I use in my recipes (e.g. basil, parsley, etc.) are the dried versions. This is really due more to convenience than anything, as fresh herbs tend to spoil in my refrigerator before I get to use all of them. I've found that as long as there is ample liquid in a recipe, the dried herbs will hydrate adequately and release their flavor. If, however, you prefer to use fresh herbs, feel free. You might want to do a quick internet search to find a conversion for fresh versus dried herbs though, as some dried seasonings (e.g. garlic powder) may require a different recipe quantity than their fresh counterparts.

- When using dried spice (and some herb) products, be sure to check the Nutrition Facts label on *all* of them for sodium content. Chili powder, as one example, can be packaged as sodium-free or may include a significant amount of sodium (e.g. 110mg per ⅛th tsp), depending upon the brand. In this cookbook, all herb and spice ingredients contain zero sodium.

Low-sodium ingredient options:

- As detailed in the ingredient list, many recipes in this cookbook call for reduced-sodium ingredients like bacon or soy sauce, and I recommend seeking out these lower-sodium options when possible. The Nutrition Facts panel reflects the sodium content for these products, so if you use the traditional (i.e. non-reduced-sodium) ingredient version, be sure to adjust the sodium level accordingly. You may also have access to low-sodium options for some ingredients (e.g. Worcestershire sauce) which are not mentioned in this book. If that is an option for you, use those products and reap an additional low-sodium advantage!

Sodium-free ingredients:

- Alongside the reduced-sodium ingredients, many of the recipes you'll find in this cookbook contain ingredients that are not traditionally sodium free. Examples include chicken and beef broth, ketchup, and baking powder. The reduction in sodium intake that results from using these sodium-free options can be immense. For example, the sodium content for traditional ketchup can be 160mg per tablespoon or more, while traditional baking powder can have sodium levels of 60mg or more per ⅛th teaspoon. The tradeoff for these sodium-free products is that they can be difficult to find in your local stores. When you can't find these sodium-free options locally, a quick internet search will often reveal several options for you.

A few notes about specific ingredients:

Carrots: you'll find that many of my recipes call for grated or shaved carrots. When a recipe traditionally calls for diced, chopped, or sliced carrots, my common practice is to bring out my peeler and shave some carrot into the pot or skillet. I find it faster and easier than pulling out a knife and cutting board and slicing or dicing a carrot. For most all recipes, your preferred carrot style – diced, chopped, sliced, julienned – will substitute just fine for my instructions of 'grated or shaved' carrot, though there can be slight changes in the total amount of the item used. For example, 1 cup of grated carrot weighs around 3.9 ounces while 1 cup of chopped carrot weighs about 4.5 ounces which can result in slight variations in the total nutritional content for some recipes.

Cooking oil: The amount of cooking oil used to fry a food is much more than what is actually consumed. Calculating the actual amount consumed can be quite challenging as not all cooking oil gets absorbed into the food yet some does make it into the breading. The actual amount of oil absorbed depends upon factors such as the type of breading used, the composition of the food itself, and even the temperature of the oil. To account for the understanding that some oil will be consumed, for those recipes in which oil is used for frying, the nutrition information is calculated based on the inclusion of 2 tablespoons of oil.

Diced tomatoes: A lot of my recipes call for diced tomatoes, including soups as well as certain sauces. For many of these recipes, I prefer a that the sauce is smooth rather than full of chunky tomatoes. Using tomato sauce is one option, but over time I've come to prefer a texture that tomato sauce doesn't provide. To me, canned, crushed tomatoes are preferrable for these sauces, but in my local area the only no-salt-added version of crushed tomatoes is the more expensive 'organic' version. Therefore, I will often put the canned diced tomatoes through a spin in my food processor to purée them before adding to the recipe. As a result, many of my recipes will call for *no-salt-added tomatoes, diced and puréed*, but whether or not you choose to purée them will have no bearing on the sodium content.

Marinades and breading: It's difficult to calculate the Nutrition Facts for a recipe that involves breading the chicken wings or marinating the steak since there's no guarantee of how much of each marinade or breading will actually be consumed. For example, when marinating meat it is common to have quite a bit of the marinade left over when removing the meat for cooking. That leftover portion includes a lot of the sodium that is inherent to many traditional marinades. Similarly, it's expected that you will have some breading material left over once the recipe has been prepared. To be completely accurate in calculating the sodium in this leftover marinade would require a lot of tedious weighing and measuring after the food has been prepared. Therefore, to address this issue I've made some assumptions in the Nutrition Facts panel. In this cookbook, items like marinade or breading (e.g. flour, breadcrumbs, etc.) have a low sodium content to begin with. Therefore, I have included *all* marinade and breading ingredients in each recipe's Nutrition Facts calculation. This will, of course, add significantly to some items listed on the Nutrition Facts label such as calories and carbohydrates. If in preparing a recipe you end up with some marinade or breading left over, feel free to adjust the Nutrition Facts information based upon the quantity of marinade or breading you did not consume.

Yellow onions: If I have a recipe that calls for ground beef, I almost always include '*yellow onion, diced*' – and often include a lot of it. You may not be as big of a fan, or you may like white onions over yellow. Feel free to reduce the amount of yellow onion that many of my recipes call for, or substitute with any other onion type when needed.

Entrées

Baked Chicken Tetrazzini

Prep Time: 20 Cook Time: 30 Recipe quantity:

INGREDIENTS

- 16oz spaghetti
- 6 tbsp unsalted butter, divided
- 1 tsp garlic powder
- 2 cups (6oz) mushrooms, sliced
- ½ cup white wine
- ¼ cup all-purpose flour
- 2 ½ cups no-salt-added chicken broth
- 1 cup heavy cream
- 4 cups (~22oz) skinless cooked chicken breast, shredded
- 1 cup shredded white cheddar cheese
- 1 cup (4oz) frozen peas
- 1 tsp dried oregano
- ½ tsp black pepper
- 1 cup unseasoned breadcrumbs
- ½ cup Parmesan cheese
- 2 tbsp olive oil

Nutrition Facts	
Serving size	
Amount Per Serving	
Calories	5420
	% Daily Value*
Total Fat 250g	**321%**
Saturated Fat 122g	**610%**
Trans Fat 0g	
Cholesterol 895mg	**298%**
Sodium 1700mg	**74%**
Total Carbohydrate 464g	**169%**
Dietary Fiber 39g	**139%**
Total Sugars 37g	
Includes 2g Added Sugars	**4%**
Protein 270g	**540%**
Vitamin D 16mcg	80%
Calcium 1495mg	110%
Iron 25mg	140%
Potassium 4814mg	100%

*The % Daily Value (DV) tells you how much a nutrient in a serving of food contributes to a daily diet. 2,000 calories a day is used for general nutrition advice.

DIRECTIONS

Preheat oven to 350°. Cook the spaghetti according to the package directions, then drain. Spray a 9"-x-13" baking dish with cooking spray. Melt 2 tbsp of butter over medium heat in a wide skillet. Add the garlic powder and cook for 1 minute, then add the mushrooms and wine and cook for 5 minutes or until the mushrooms are soft and most of the liquid has been absorbed. Add the remaining 4 tbsp of butter, then stir in the flour and cook until the flour turns a golden-brown color (~3min). Slowly add the broth and cream and whisk until no lumps remain. Simmer until thickened (~5 minutes). Stir in the chicken, cheese, peas, oregano, and black pepper, then add the cooked spaghetti and toss together. Transfer the preparation into the baking dish. In a separate small bowl, toss to combine the breadcrumbs, Parmesan, and oil, the add this mix over the top of the spaghetti preparation. Bake approximately 25 minutes, or until the Panko topping turns golden brown.

Baked Chicken Wings

Prep Time: 20 Cook Time: 45 Recipe quantity:

INGREDIENTS

- 3lbs skinless chicken wings
- 1 cup all-purpose flour
- 1 tbsp garlic powder
- 1 tbsp sodium-free chili powder
- 1 tsp cumin
- 1 tsp dried parsley
- 1 tbsp black pepper
- 3 eggs
- ¼ cup milk
- 3 cups unseasoned breadcrumbs

Nutrition Facts	
Serving size	
Amount Per Serving	
Calories	**1820**
	% Daily Value*
Total Fat 27g	**35%**
Saturated Fat 10g	**50%**
Trans Fat 0g	
Cholesterol 725mg	**242%**
Sodium 530mg	**23%**
Total Carbohydrate 241g	**88%**
Dietary Fiber 18g	**64%**
Total Sugars 15g	
Includes 0g Added Sugars	**0%**
Protein 127g	**254%**
Vitamin D 4mcg	20%
Calcium 237mg	20%
Iron 28mg	160%
Potassium 1561mg	35%

*The % Daily Value (DV) tells you how much a nutrient in a serving of food contributes to a daily diet. 2,000 calories a day is used for general nutrition advice.

DIRECTIONS

Separate the wings into individual wingettes and drumettes, discarding the tips. Set up three medium-sized bowls on the counter. In one bowl, add most of the dry ingredients: 1 cup of flour, the garlic powder, chili powder, cumin, parsley, and black pepper and stir to combine. In a separate bowl, beat the eggs with the milk. In a third bowl, add the breadcrumbs. Preheat the oven to 350°F. Dredge thoroughly in the first bowl, shaking off any extra coating. Next, dip the chicken in the egg mixture, allowing any excess to drip off. Finally, dredge thoroughly in the breadcrumb mixture and shake off any excess breadcrumbs. Line the wings up on a wire rack placed on a sheet pan, then place in the oven and bake for 45 minutes or until the internal temperature of the wings reaches 165°F. Remove from the oven and allow to rest for 5 minutes before serving.

Beef Enchiladas

Prep Time: 25 Cook Time: 30 Recipe quantity:

INGREDIENTS

Red Sauce

- **2 cups sodium-free beef broth**
- **1 tbsp cornstarch**
- **4 tbsp sodium-free chili powder**
- **½ tsp ground cumin**
- **½ tsp garlic powder**

Filling

- **1½lbs ground beef (I prefer 80:20 ground chuck)**
- **½ medium yellow onion (4oz), diced**
- **½ cup (3oz) bell pepper, diced**
- **½ tsp black pepper**
- **10 corn tortillas**
- **1 cup + ½ cup shredded cheddar cheese**

Nutrition Facts

Serving size	
Amount Per Serving	
Calories	**3100**
	% Daily Value*
Total Fat 196g	**251%**
Saturated Fat 90g	**450%**
Trans Fat 0g	
Cholesterol 660mg	**220%**
Sodium 1590mg	**69%**
Total Carbohydrate 148g	**54%**
Dietary Fiber 17g	**61%**
Total Sugars 9g	
Includes 2g Added Sugars	**4%**
Protein 176g	**352%**
Vitamin D 0mcg	0%
Calcium 1427mg	110%
Iron 20mg	110%
Potassium 3398mg	70%

*The % Daily Value (DV) tells you how much a nutrient in a serving of food contributes to a daily diet. 2,000 calories a day is used for general nutrition advice.

DIRECTIONS

Make the sauce first. In a saucepan whisk ¼ cup of beef broth with the cornstarch. Next, add the remaining beef broth, chili powder, cumin, and garlic powder. Bring to a boil, simmer covered over low heat for 4-5 minutes, stirring often. While simmering, prepare the meat filling. Brown the ground beef with the diced onion and bell pepper, then add the black pepper. Preheat oven to 350°F and lightly grease a 9"x13" oven dish. Spread ½ cup of enchilada sauce in the bottom of the dish. To assemble, coat one side of a tortilla with the remaining red sauce, then place the tortilla sauce-side-up in the baking dish. Spoon approximately ½ cup of the meat filling into the tortilla, add a pinch of cheddar cheese, then roll up the tortilla. Repeat for all 10 tortillas. Pour the remaining red sauce over the assembled tortillas, then sprinkle the ½ cup of cheddar over the top. Bake for 30 minutes or until the filling is bubbling.

Beef Fried Rice

Prep Time: 10 Cook Time: 15 Recipe quantity:

INGREDIENTS

- 2 cups instant rice
- ½lb ground beef (I prefer 80:20 ground chuck)
- ½ cup canola oil
- 2 tbsp low-sodium soy sauce
- 1 cup (4oz) frozen peas
- ¼ cup (1oz) grated or shredded carrots
- 1 tsp ground black pepper

Nutrition Facts

Serving size	
Amount Per Serving	
Calories	**2400**
	% Daily Value*
Total Fat 156g	**200%**
Saturated Fat 26g	**130%**
Trans Fat 0g	
Cholesterol 160mg	**53%**
Sodium 300mg	**13%**
Total Carbohydrate 193g	**70%**
Dietary Fiber 7g	**25%**
Total Sugars 33g	
Includes 0g Added Sugars	**0%**
Protein 66g	**132%**
Vitamin D 0mcg	0%
Calcium 60mg	4%
Iron 16mg	90%
Potassium 935mg	20%

*The % Daily Value (DV) tells you how much a nutrient in a serving of food contributes to a daily diet. 2,000 calories a day is used for general nutrition advice.

DIRECTIONS

Cook instant rice according to directions, then cool to room temperature if possible. Brown the ground beef over medium-high heat and chop into fine pieces. Heat ¼ cup of the oil in a wok or wide skillet. Cook the rice in the oil for 8-10 minutes, stirring often and adding the second ¼ cup of oil halfway through. Add soy sauce to the rice and stir, then add the peas, diced carrots, and ground pepper and cook for an additional five minutes, stirring often. Add the browned ground beef, stir to mix, then serve.

Beef Jerky

Prep Time: 15 Cook Time: varied Recipe quantity:

INGREDIENTS

- 2lbs top round or other lean beef, cut into ⅛"-thick strips
- 1 cup water
- ¼ cup low-sodium soy sauce
- 2 tbsp liquid smoke
- 2 tbsp brown sugar
- 2 tsp black pepper
- 1 tsp cumin
- ½ tsp garlic powder
- ½ tsp onion powder

Nutrition Facts

Nutrition Facts	
Serving size	
Amount Per Serving	
Calories	**1160**
	% Daily Value*
Total Fat 56g	**72%**
Saturated Fat 24g	**120%**
Trans Fat 0g	
Cholesterol 560mg	**187%**
Sodium 740mg	**32%**
Total Carbohydrate 84g	**31%**
Dietary Fiber 0g	**0%**
Total Sugars 76g	
Includes 0g Added Sugars	**0%**
Protein 285g	**570%**
Vitamin D 0mcg	0%
Calcium 223mg	15%
Iron 22mg	120%
Potassium 40mg	0%

*The % Daily Value (DV) tells you how much a nutrient in a serving of food contributes to a daily diet. 2,000 calories a day is used for general nutrition advice.

DIRECTIONS

In a small bowl, mix the water, soy sauce, liquid smoke, and all spices together and mix well. Place the beef strips into a large freezer-type (or other sealable) bag and pour in the spice mixture. Knead the meat in the bag to incorporate the marinade, then place in a refrigerator overnight. Using a home dehydrator appliance, place the strips as required for the dehydrator without allowing the pieces to touch. Dehydrate according to manufacturer's directions.

Beef and Potato Stroganoff

Prep Time: 20 Cook Time: 40 Recipe quantity:

INGREDIENTS

- 1lb ground beef (I prefer 80:20 ground chuck)
- ½ medium yellow onion (4oz), diced
- 2 tbsp olive oil
- ½ cup (2oz) carrot, grated or shredded
- 3 cups sodium-free beef broth
- ½ tsp garlic powder
- ½ tsp black pepper
- 2 cups thinly sliced red or Russet potatoes
- 2 tbsp Worcestershire sauce
- 1 cup (4oz) frozen peas
- 1 tbsp corn starch
- ¼ cup water
- ½ cup sour cream

Nutrition Facts

Serving size	
Amount Per Serving	
Calories	**2140**
	% Daily Value*
Total Fat 128g	**164%**
Saturated Fat 47g	**235%**
Trans Fat 0g	
Cholesterol 360mg	**120%**
Sodium 830mg	**36%**
Total Carbohydrate 145g	**53%**
Dietary Fiber 17g	**61%**
Total Sugars 30g	
Includes 3g Added Sugars	**6%**
Protein 102g	**204%**
Vitamin D 0mcg	0%
Calcium 277mg	20%
Iron 17mg	90%
Potassium 5244mg	110%

*The % Daily Value (DV) tells you how much a nutrient in a serving of food contributes to a daily diet. 2,000 calories a day is used for general nutrition advice.

DIRECTIONS

In a large skillet, brown the ground beef over medium-high heat along with the diced onion. Drain and remove the meat/onion mix to a bowl. In same skillet add the olive oil and then cook the carrot for 2-3 minutes or until it is cooked through. Add the beef broth, garlic powder, pepper, cooked ground beef and onions, sliced potatoes, Worcestershire sauce, and green peas. Bring to a boil then cover and simmer for 25 minutes. Mix the cornstarch and water, and after the simmer time is up, add the corn starch mixture to the skillet, stir thoroughly, then turn off the heat and stir in the sour cream. Allow to rest for five minutes before serving.

Beef Stew

Prep Time: 20 Cook Time: 140 Recipe quantity:

INGREDIENTS

- 1 tbsp olive oil
- 1lb chuck roast or sirloin, cut into 1" cubes
- 2 tbsp all-purpose flour
- 4 cups sodium-free beef broth
- ½ cup (2oz) carrot, shredded
- 1 cup (4oz) frozen peas
- 1 med. yellow onion (8oz), chopped
- 1 med. bell pepper (~6oz), chopped
- 2 cups (~10oz) red potatoes, chopped
- 1 (14.5oz) can no-salt-added diced tomatoes
- 1 (8oz) can no-salt-added tomato sauce
- 2 tbsp Worcestershire sauce
- 1 tsp ground black pepper
- 1 tsp paprika
- 1 tsp cumin
- ½ tsp garlic powder
- ½ tsp onion powder
- 2 tsp corn starch
- ¼ cup water

Nutrition Facts	
Serving size	
Amount Per Serving	
Calories	**1320**
	% Daily Value*
Total Fat 43g	**55%**
Saturated Fat 14g	**70%**
Trans Fat 0g	
Cholesterol 280mg	**93%**
Sodium 850mg	**37%**
Total Carbohydrate 163g	**59%**
Dietary Fiber 27g	**96%**
Total Sugars 52g	
Includes 4g Added Sugars	**8%**
Protein 170g	**340%**
Vitamin D 0mcg	0%
Calcium 276mg	20%
Iron 19mg	110%
Potassium 5344mg	110%

*The % Daily Value (DV) tells you how much a nutrient in a serving of food contributes to a daily diet. 2,000 calories a day is used for general nutrition advice.

DIRECTIONS

Heat the olive oil over medium-high heat in a medium-sized skillet. Place the flour and meat in a plastic bag and shake vigorously to coat the meat with flour. Working in batches, transfer the meat to the skillet, browning on all sides. While browning, place the remaining ingredients (up through the onion powder) into a large soup pot. Bring to a boil, then simmer. Once the meat is browned, add it to the pot. Add ½ cup of liquid from the Dutch oven to the skillet and scrape any remaining bits of meat from the bottom of the pan, then add the liquid back to the Dutch oven. Cover, and cook for approximately 2 hours at a slow simmer, stirring occasionally. 5 minutes before serving, mix the cornstarch and water in a small bowl, then stir this mixture into the soup pot.

Beef Stir Fry

Prep Time: 20 Cook Time: 15 Recipe quantity:

INGREDIENTS

- ¼ cup olive oil
- 1 tbsp Worcestershire sauce
- 3 tbsp low-sodium soy sauce, divided
- ½ tsp garlic powder
- ½ tsp onion powder
- ¾lb ribeye or other steak meat, sliced into ¼" thick by 2" slices
- ¼ cup canola oil, divided
- ½ cup (2oz) carrots, grated or sliced
- 2 cups (5oz) broccoli florets
- 2 cups (5oz) cauliflower florets
- 2 cups instant rice

Nutrition Facts

Serving size

Amount Per Serving	
Calories	**2760**
	% Daily Value*
Total Fat 189g	**242%**
Saturated Fat 25g	**125%**
Trans Fat 0g	
Cholesterol 210mg	**70%**
Sodium 800mg	**35%**
Total Carbohydrate 227g	**83%**
Dietary Fiber 15g	**54%**
Total Sugars 56g	
Includes 0g Added Sugars	**0%**
Protein 137g	**274%**
Vitamin D 0mcg	0%
Calcium 295mg	25%
Iron 12mg	70%
Potassium 1971mg	40%

*The % Daily Value (DV) tells you how much a nutrient in a serving of food contributes to a daily diet. 2,000 calories a day is used for general nutrition advice.

DIRECTIONS

Make the marinade by combining the olive oil, Worcestershire sauce, 1 tbsp soy sauce, garlic powder, and onion powder. Place the steak slices in a bag or bowl, add the marinade, and mix to coat. Place in the refrigerator for at least one hour. Heat 1 tbsp of canola oil in a large skillet or wok over medium-high heat. Add the (drained) steak and stir often until cooked through (7-10 min). Remove the meat and discard the liquid, then add the remaining canola oil. Once the oil has heated, add the carrots, broccoli, and cauliflower, stirring often. While the vegetables are cooking, prepare and cook the instant rice according to package instructions. Cook the vegetables on high heat until slightly tender, approximately 7-8 minutes. In the last minute of cooking, sprinkle the remaining 2 tbsp soy sauce over the vegetables and then add the cooked steak. Cook for an additional minute then serve over the rice.

Beef Tips

Prep Time: 15   Cook Time: 45   Recipe quantity:

INGREDIENTS

- 1 tbsp olive oil
- 2lbs round steak or sirloin, cut into ½" cubes
- 1 tbsp unsalted butter
- 1 medium yellow onion (8oz), diced
- ¼ cup all-purpose flour
- 1 tsp garlic powder
- 4 cups sodium-free beef broth
- 2 tbsp low-sodium soy sauce
- 2 tbsp Worcestershire sauce
- 1 tbsp dried parsley
- 1 tsp black pepper
- 1 tsp dried thyme

Nutrition Facts

Serving size	
Amount Per Serving	
Calories	**1380**
	% Daily Value*
Total Fat 81g	**104%**
Saturated Fat 30g	**150%**
Trans Fat 0g	
Cholesterol 575mg	**192%**
Sodium 1000mg	**43%**
Total Carbohydrate 75g	**27%**
Dietary Fiber 4g	**14%**
Total Sugars 39g	
Includes 4g Added Sugars	**8%**
Protein 289g	**578%**
Vitamin D 0mcg	0%
Calcium 271mg	20%
Iron 25mg	140%
Potassium 1558mg	35%

*The % Daily Value (DV) tells you how much a nutrient in a serving of food contributes to a daily diet. 2,000 calories a day is used for general nutrition advice.

DIRECTIONS

In a wide skillet, heat 2 tbsp of the olive oil over medium-high heat. Add the cubed steak pieces and cook for 6-7 minutes, stirring occasionally. Once seared, move the steak pieces to a plate. In the same skillet, melt the butter and add the onions. Cook until the onions turn translucent (~5-7 minutes). Add the flour and garlic powder to the skillet and cook for 2 minutes, stirring often, until the flour turns a light brown color. Add the remaining ingredients and then stir to mix. Add the steak pieces back in, bring to a boil, then reduce to a simmer and cook uncovered for 30-35 minutes, stirring occasionally. Serve alone or over rice.

Bierocks

Prep Time: 45 Cook Time: 30 Recipe quantity:

INGREDIENTS

Dough

- **1 envelope active dry yeast**
- **¼ cup lukewarm water**
- **1 cup warm milk (~120°F)**
- **1/3 cup granulated sugar**
- **¼ cup unsalted butter, + 1 tbsp**
- **1 egg, lightly beaten**
- **4 ½ cups all-purpose flour**

Filling

- **2lbs ground beef (I prefer 80:20 ground chuck)**
- **1 medium yellow onion (8oz), diced**
- **1½ cups (~5oz) cabbage, diced**
- **1 cup shredded cheddar cheese**

Nutrition Facts

Serving size	
Amount Per Serving	
Calories	**5310**
	% Daily Value*
Total Fat 280g	**359%**
Saturated Fat 123g	**615%**
Trans Fat 0g	
Cholesterol 1055mg	**352%**
Sodium 1490mg	**65%**
Total Carbohydrate 432g	**157%**
Dietary Fiber 57g	**204%**
Total Sugars 22g	
Includes 0g Added Sugars	**0%**
Protein 251g	**502%**
Vitamin D 3mcg	15%
Calcium 1299mg	100%
Iron 40mg	220%
Potassium 5299mg	110%

*The % Daily Value (DV) tells you how much a nutrient in a serving of food contributes to a daily diet. 2,000 calories a day is used for general nutrition advice.

DIRECTIONS

In a small bowl, mix the yeast and water and set aside. To the warm milk, add the sugar and the 1/4 cup butter and stir until the sugar dissolves. Add the milk mixture to the yeast, then add the egg. Place these mixed ingredients into your stand mixer bowl. Over slow speed, add one cup of flour at a time to the bowl. Once incorporated, remove the dough and knead on a counter for 3-4 minutes. Grease a large bowl and place the dough in the bowl, then cover with cellophane or a damp paper towel. Allow to rise for 1 - 2 hours. To make the filling, brown the ground beef with the onion. With five minutes left, drain the meat and add the cabbage, stirring often. Preheat the oven to 375°F. To assemble, roll a 1" ball of dough into a 6" circle. Spoon ¼ cup of meat mixture into the center, then add a pinch of cheddar cheese and close up the dough. Repeat until the dough or meat mixture has been used up. Melt the 1 tbsp of butter and brush onto each bierock top. Bake for 20-25 minutes until the tops are golden brown.

Broccoli Chicken Pasta

Prep Time: 15 Cook Time: 30 Recipe quantity:

INGREDIENTS

- **1 tbsp olive oil**
- **2 cups skinless chicken breast (~10oz), cut into ¾" cubes**
- **1 medium yellow onion (8oz), diced**
- **½ tsp garlic powder**
- **12oz pasta, uncooked**
- **1 cup sodium-free chicken broth**
- **2 cups milk**
- **2 cups (5oz) broccoli florets, chopped**
- **¼ tsp cumin**
- **1½ cups shredded cheddar cheese**

Nutrition Facts

Serving size	
Amount Per Serving	
Calories	**2890**
	% Daily Value*
Total Fat 100g	**128%**
Saturated Fat 51g	**255%**
Trans Fat 0g	
Cholesterol 410mg	**137%**
Sodium 1380mg	**60%**
Total Carbohydrate 313g	**114%**
Dietary Fiber 25g	**89%**
Total Sugars 39g	
Includes 1g Added Sugars	**2%**
Protein 178g	**356%**
Vitamin D 4mcg	20%
Calcium 2025mg	160%
Iron 17mg	90%
Potassium 3597mg	80%

*The % Daily Value (DV) tells you how much a nutrient in a serving of food contributes to a daily diet. 2,000 calories a day is used for general nutrition advice.

DIRECTIONS

In a soup pot or Dutch oven, heat the olive oil over medium heat and add the chicken and onion. Cook until the chicken has cooked through, approximately 8-10 minutes. Add the garlic powder, pasta, chicken broth, and milk, bring to a near boil, then cover and reduce the heat to a simmer for 10-12 minutes or until the pasta begins to soften, stirring occasionally. Stir in the broccoli florets and allow to simmer for 5 minutes uncovered. When the liquid is nearly gone, add the cumin and the cheddar cheese and stir to incorporate. Once the cheese has melted, remove from the heat and allow to rest for 5 minutes prior to serving.

Catfish Nuggets

Prep Time: 15 Cook Time: 25 Recipe quantity:

INGREDIENTS

- 1lb catfish fillets, cut into 1" squares
- 1 cup all-purpose flour
- 1 tsp garlic powder
- 1 tsp black pepper
- 1 tsp paprika
- ¼ cup milk
- 2 eggs
- 2 cups corn meal
- 3 cups canola oil (for frying)

Nutrition Facts

Serving size	
Amount Per Serving	
Calories	**2300**
	% Daily Value*
Total Fat 54g	**69%**
Saturated Fat 11g	**55%**
Trans Fat 0g	
Cholesterol 405mg	**135%**
Sodium 240mg	**10%**
Total Carbohydrate 419g	**152%**
Dietary Fiber 28g	**100%**
Total Sugars 12g	
Includes 0g Added Sugars	**0%**
Protein 63g	**126%**
Vitamin D 4mcg	20%
Calcium 379mg	30%
Iron 12mg	70%
Potassium 2544mg	50%

*The % Daily Value (DV) tells you how much a nutrient in a serving of food contributes to a daily diet. 2,000 calories a day is used for general nutrition advice.

DIRECTIONS

Set up three bowls for dredging. In the first bowl, place the flour, garlic powder, black pepper, and paprika and stir to combine. In the 2nd bowl, mix the eggs with the milk. In the 3rd bowl, place the corn meal. In a wide skillet, heat the canola oil to approximately 350°F. Coat the fillet pieces in the flour mix, then shake off the excess. Next, dip them in the egg mixture, ensuring even coating. Finally, coat them with the corn meal. Place each coated nugget into the hot oil and fry for approximately 2-3 minutes per side or until cooked through (time depends upon the thickness of your fillet).

Cheeseburger Macaroni

Prep Time: 30 Cook Time: 10 Recipe quantity:

INGREDIENTS

- 1lb ground beef (I prefer 80:20 ground chuck)
- ½ medium yellow onion (4oz), chopped
- 3 cups sodium-free beef broth
- ½ cup sodium-free ketchup
- 2 tbsp no-salt-added tomato paste
- 1 tsp garlic powder
- ½ tsp black pepper
- 12 ounces rotini or penne pasta
- 3 tbsp unsalted butter
- 3 tbsp all-purpose flour
- 1 cup milk
- 1 ½ cups shredded cheddar cheese

Nutrition Facts

Serving size	
Amount Per Serving	
Calories	**3840**
	% Daily Value*
Total Fat 189g	**242%**
Saturated Fat 89g	**445%**
Trans Fat 0g	
Cholesterol 580mg	**193%**
Sodium 1510mg	**66%**
Total Carbohydrate 358g	**130%**
Dietary Fiber 23g	**82%**
Total Sugars 71g	
Includes 35g Added Sugars	**70%**
Protein 177g	**354%**
Vitamin D 2mcg	10%
Calcium 1639mg	130%
Iron 25mg	140%
Potassium 5133mg	110%

*The % Daily Value (DV) tells you how much a nutrient in a serving of food contributes to a daily diet. 2,000 calories a day is used for general nutrition advice.

DIRECTIONS

In a large skillet, brown the ground beef over medium-high heat along with the onion. Add the broth, ketchup, tomato paste, garlic powder and black pepper. Stir to combine the ingredients, then bring to a boil. Add the pasta, pushing it into the liquid, then cover and reduce the heat to a simmer. In a separate medium skillet over medium-high heat, prepare the sauce. Melt the butter then slowly stir in the flour. Once the flour begins to brown, slowly whisk in the milk. Once mixed, cook until nearly boiling while stirring constantly (~3-4 minutes). Reduce the heat to medium-low, then add the cheese in batches while stirring constantly. Once all the cheese has been incorporated and the sauce is smooth, turn off the heat. Once the liquid has been absorbed in the pasta skillet, add the cheese sauce and stir to incorporate. Turn off the heat and allow to rest for 5 minutes before serving.

Cheesy Beef Pasta

Prep Time: 10 Cook Time: 20 Recipe quantity:

INGREDIENTS

- 1lb ground beef (I prefer 80:20 ground chuck)
- ¾ medium yellow onion (6oz), diced
- ½ tsp black pepper
- 1 tsp garlic powder
- 4 cups sodium-free chicken broth
- 16oz dried pasta (I prefer rotini)
- ¾ cup heavy whipping cream
- 1 ½ cups shredded cheddar cheese
- ½ cup Parmesan cheese

Nutrition Facts

Serving size	
Amount Per Serving	
Calories	**4280**
	% Daily Value*
Total Fat 222g	**285%**
Saturated Fat 122g	**610%**
Trans Fat 0g	
Cholesterol 780mg	**260%**
Sodium 1990mg	**87%**
Total Carbohydrate 377g	**137%**
Dietary Fiber 25g	**89%**
Total Sugars 27g	
Includes 4g Added Sugars	**8%**
Protein 196g	**392%**
Vitamin D 0mcg	0%
Calcium 1888mg	150%
Iron 29mg	160%
Potassium 4157mg	90%

*The % Daily Value (DV) tells you how much a nutrient in a serving of food contributes to a daily diet. 2,000 calories a day is used for general nutrition advice.

DIRECTIONS

In a large skillet, brown the ground beef over medium-high heat along with the onion. Add the black pepper, garlic powder, chicken broth, and pasta. Bring to a boil, then cover and simmer for 15 minutes or until the pasta has cooked through, stirring often to ensure the pasta contacts the liquid. If needed, add some more water until the pasta reaches the desired consistency. Once the pasta is ready, uncover and stir in the heavy cream, then add the cheddar cheese in batches, stirring constantly to incorporate. Once the cheddar cheese has melted, turn off the heat and stir in the Parmesan cheese. Allow to rest for 5 minutes prior to serving.

Chicken and Dumplings

Prep Time: 20 Cook Time: 60 Recipe quantity:

INGREDIENTS

- 3 cups (15oz) skinless chicken breast
- 1 medium yellow onion (8oz), chopped
- ½ cup (2oz) carrots, grated or shredded
- 1/3 cup (~1.5oz) celery, diced
- 1 tsp black pepper
- 6 cups sodium-free chicken broth
- *Buttermilk biscuit recipe (make through the dough preparation)

Nutrition Facts	
Serving size	
Amount Per Serving	
Calories	2750
	% Daily Value*
Total Fat 103g	132%
Saturated Fat 37g	185%
Trans Fat 0g	
Cholesterol 450mg	150%
Sodium 360mg	16%
Total Carbohydrate 229g	83%
Dietary Fiber 28g	100%
Total Sugars 35g	
Includes 6g Added Sugars	12%
Protein 179g	358%
Vitamin D 2mcg	10%
Calcium 1276mg	100%
Iron 15mg	80%
Potassium 7187mg	150%

*The % Daily Value (DV) tells you how much a nutrient in a serving of food contributes to a daily diet. 2,000 calories a day is used for general nutrition advice.

DIRECTIONS

In a soup pot, add the chicken breasts, onion, carrots, celery, black pepper, and chicken broth. Bring to a boil, then reduce to a simmer and cook covered for 1 hour. While cooking, prepare the Buttermilk Biscuit recipe (see Breakfast section) but do not bake the biscuits - only prepare the dough. After simmering the chicken for 1 hour, remove the breasts to a cutting board and shred, then return the shredded chicken to the pot. With 10 minutes left in the cooking time, add 20-25 1" balls of the buttermilk biscuit dough to the pot, allowing the dough to cook in the pot (freeze any remaining dough or prepare biscuits separately), stirring occasionally.

Chicken Carbonara

Prep Time: 15 Cook Time: 25 Recipe quantity:

INGREDIENTS

- 16 ounces uncooked spaghetti
- 4 slices low-sodium bacon, diced
- 3 cups (15oz) skinless chicken breast, cut into thin 1" strips
- ¼ cup (1oz) green onion, diced
- ½ tsp garlic powder
- 3 eggs
- ¼ cup Parmesan cheese
- ½ tsp black pepper
- 1 tbsp dried parsley
- ¼ cup reserved pasta water

Nutrition Facts

Serving size	
Amount Per Serving	
Calories	**2720**
	% Daily Value*
Total Fat 51g	**65%**
Saturated Fat 18g	**90%**
Trans Fat 0g	
Cholesterol 835mg	**278%**
Sodium 950mg	**41%**
Total Carbohydrate 339g	**123%**
Dietary Fiber 25g	**89%**
Total Sugars 10g	
Includes 0g Added Sugars	**0%**
Protein 200g	**400%**
Vitamin D 3mcg	15%
Calcium 449mg	35%
Iron 24mg	130%
Potassium 2453mg	50%

*The % Daily Value (DV) tells you how much a nutrient in a serving of food contributes to a daily diet. 2,000 calories a day is used for general nutrition advice.

DIRECTIONS

Cook the spaghetti according to package directions, reserving ¼ cup of the pasta water before draining. In a large skillet, cook the bacon until just crispy, then remove it from the pan, leaving ~1 tbsp of bacon grease in the skillet. Add the chicken breast. Cook the chicken for ~8 minutes or until cooked through, stirring often. Add the green onion and cook for an additional 2 minutes. In a separate bowl, mix together the garlic powder, eggs, Parmesan cheese, black pepper, parsley, and the ¼ cup of reserved pasta water. Remove the chicken and green onion from the skillet and drain all but approximately 2 tbsp of liquid from the skillet. Add the pasta to the skillet. Over low heat, add the egg mixture to the pasta, tossing the mixture constantly and adding the reserved pasta water until the desired sauce thickness is reached. Mix the bacon with the chicken and add to the pasta. Cook for an additional 2 minutes, then serve.

Chicken Cheese Nuggets

Prep Time: 20 Cook Time: 15 Recipe quantity:

INGREDIENTS

- 2 cups (10oz) cooked skinless chicken breasts, diced
- 3 eggs, beaten
- ¼ cup all-purpose flour
- 1¾ cups shredded mozzarella cheese
- ½ medium yellow onion (4oz), minced
- ½ tsp paprika
- 1 tsp dried rosemary
- ½ tsp garlic powder
- ½ tsp cumin
- ½ tsp black pepper
- 1 cup unseasoned breadcrumbs
- 3 cups canola or vegetable oil for frying

Nutrition Facts

Serving size	
Amount Per Serving	
Calories	**1700**
	% Daily Value*
Total Fat 85g	**109%**
Saturated Fat 28g	**140%**
Trans Fat 0g	
Cholesterol 485mg	**162%**
Sodium 1560mg	**68%**
Total Carbohydrate 92g	**33%**
Dietary Fiber 6g	**21%**
Total Sugars 6g	
Includes 0g Added Sugars	**0%**
Protein 137g	**274%**
Vitamin D 1mcg	4%
Calcium 1477mg	110%
Iron 9mg	50%
Potassium 1437mg	30%

*The % Daily Value (DV) tells you how much a nutrient in a serving of food contributes to a daily diet. 2,000 calories a day is used for general nutrition advice.

DIRECTIONS

In a large mixing bowl add all ingredients through the black pepper and mix well. In a second bowl, add the breadcrumbs. Take approximately 1 tbsp of the mixture and roll it into a ball, then flatten slightly. Place the flattened ball in the breadcrumbs and coat thoroughly. In a medium skillet, heat the oil to 350°F. Fry each nugget for approximately 3 minutes per side or until cooked through.

Chicken Fried Steak

Prep Time: 25 Cook Time: 20 Recipe quantity:

INGREDIENTS

- 1lb cube steak, tenderized
- 1 cup all-purpose flour + 2 cups
- 1 tsp cumin
- 1 tsp garlic powder
- 1 tsp onion powder
- 3 eggs
- 1 cup milk
- 1 tbsp sodium-free baking powder
- 1 tbsp black pepper
- 1 ½ cups canola oil for frying

Gravy

- 3 tbsp unsalted butter
- 4 tbsp all-purpose flour
- 1½ cups sodium-free beef broth
- 1 cup milk
- 2 tsp black pepper

Nutrition Facts	
Serving size	
Amount Per Serving	
Calories	2810
	% Daily Value*
Total Fat 120g	**154%**
Saturated Fat 42g	**210%**
Trans Fat 0g	
Cholesterol 950mg	**317%**
Sodium 680mg	**30%**
Total Carbohydrate 321g	**117%**
Dietary Fiber 39g	**139%**
Total Sugars 26g	
Includes 0g Added Sugars	**0%**
Protein 214g	**428%**
Vitamin D 7mcg	35%
Calcium 1814mg	140%
Iron 40mg	220%
Potassium 4735mg	100%

*The % Daily Value (DV) tells you how much a nutrient in a serving of food contributes to a daily diet. 2,000 calories a day is used for general nutrition advice.

DIRECTIONS

Set up three medium bowls. In the first, mix 1 cup flour, cumin, garlic powder, and onion powder. In the second bowl whisk the eggs and milk. In the third, mix 2 cups flour, baking powder, and black pepper. Heat the oil to 350°F. Dredge each steak in the flour and spices, then the egg wash, then the second flour bowl. Place carefully in the oil and fry for approximately 4-5 minutes per side or the internal temperature of the steak reaches 160°F. Repeat for all steaks. For the gravy, drain the oil from the pan but leave any remaining steak bits. Add the butter to the pan over medium heat. Once melted, add the flour in batches, whisking constantly. Once the flour begins to turn light brown, whisk in the beef broth. Once incorporated and all lumps are gone, slowly add the milk and then the black pepper, whisking constantly. Simmer over low heat until the desired consistency is reached.

Chicken Noodle Soup

Prep Time: 25 Cook Time: 60 Recipe quantity:

INGREDIENTS

- ½ cup water
- 2 cups (10oz) skinless chicken breast
- 6 cups sodium-free chicken broth
- 1 tsp garlic powder
- 1 tsp black pepper
- 1/3 cup (~ 1.5oz) celery, diced
- ¼ cup (1oz) carrot, grated or shredded
- 1 tsp dried basil
- ½ medium yellow onion (4oz), diced or chopped
- 16oz penne, rotini, or other short pasta

Nutrition Facts

Serving size

Amount Per Serving	
Calories	**2180**
	% Daily Value*
Total Fat 18g	**23%**
Saturated Fat 3g	**15%**
Trans Fat 0g	
Cholesterol 160mg	**53%**
Sodium 150mg	**7%**
Total Carbohydrate 358g	**130%**
Dietary Fiber 26g	**93%**
Total Sugars 18g	
Includes 6g Added Sugars	**12%**
Protein 134g	**268%**
Vitamin D 0mcg	0%
Calcium 158mg	10%
Iron 22mg	120%
Potassium 4247mg	90%

*The % Daily Value (DV) tells you how much a nutrient in a serving of food contributes to a daily diet. 2,000 calories a day is used for general nutrition advice.

DIRECTIONS

In a small skillet, add the ½ cup of water and then cook the breasts five minutes on each side or until cooked through. While the chicken is cooking, add the broth to a medium to large soup pot and bring to boil, then simmer and add the garlic powder, black pepper, diced celery, carrot, basil, and onion. Simmer for 45 minutes. When the chicken breast is done, place on a cutting board and shred, then add to the soup pot. With 15 minutes left in the broth cook time, cook the pasta according to package directions. Drain the pasta, then add to the soup pot. Simmer for 2-3 minutes before serving.

Chicken Pasta

Prep Time: 15 Cook Time: 25 Recipe quantity:

INGREDIENTS

- **1 tbsp unsalted butter**
- **3 cups (15oz) skinless chicken breast, cut into ¾" cubes**
- **½ medium yellow onion (4oz), diced**
- **1/3 cup (~1.5oz) celery, diced**
- **¼ cup (1oz) carrot, grated or shredded**
- **½ tsp black pepper**
- **1 tbsp all-purpose flour**
- **½ cup white wine**
- **4 cups sodium-free chicken broth**
- **16 oz uncooked pasta**
- **1 cup (4oz) frozen peas**
- **½ tsp dried rosemary**
- **1 tbsp dried parsley**

Nutrition Facts

Serving size	
Amount Per Serving	
Calories	**2760**
	% Daily Value*
Total Fat 34g	**44%**
Saturated Fat 8g	**40%**
Trans Fat 0g	
Cholesterol 260mg	**87%**
Sodium 250mg	**11%**
Total Carbohydrate 387g	**141%**
Dietary Fiber 35g	**125%**
Total Sugars 26g	
Includes 4g Added Sugars	**8%**
Protein 176g	**352%**
Vitamin D 0mcg	0%
Calcium 235mg	20%
Iron 24mg	130%
Potassium 4534mg	100%

*The % Daily Value (DV) tells you how much a nutrient in a serving of food contributes to a daily diet. 2,000 calories a day is used for general nutrition advice.

DIRECTIONS

In a soup pot or Dutch oven, heat the butter over medium heat and add the chicken, onion, celery, and carrot. Cook until the chicken has cooked through, approximately 8-10 minutes. Sprinkle the pepper and flour over the chicken and vegetables, stir to incorporate, then cook for one minute. Add the white wine, chicken broth, and pasta. Bring to a boil, then simmer covered for 8-10 minutes, stirring occasionally, until the pasta begins to soften and the liquid gets mostly absorbed. Add the peas, rosemary, and parsley, and cook for an additional five minutes. Turn off the heat and allow to rest for 5 minutes prior to serving.

Chicken Salad

Prep Time: 10 Cook Time: 15 Recipe quantity:

INGREDIENTS

- **2½ cups (~12oz) shredded, cooked, skinless chicken breast (chilled)**
- **¾ cup (~2.5oz) celery, diced**
- **1 cup (~6oz) seedless grapes, halved**
- **½ cup (2oz) walnuts, chopped**
- **½ medium red onion (4oz), diced**
- **1 tsp Worcestershire sauce**
- **½ cup mayonnaise**

Nutrition Facts

Serving size	
Amount Per Serving	
Calories	**1800**
	% Daily Value*
Total Fat 134g	**172%**
Saturated Fat 18g	**90%**
Trans Fat 0g	
Cholesterol 240mg	**80%**
Sodium 950mg	**41%**
Total Carbohydrate 47g	**17%**
Dietary Fiber 8g	**29%**
Total Sugars 32g	
Includes 0g Added Sugars	**0%**
Protein 80g	**160%**
Vitamin D 0mcg	0%
Calcium 137mg	10%
Iron 3mg	15%
Potassium 1565mg	35%

*The % Daily Value (DV) tells you how much a nutrient in a serving of food contributes to a daily diet. 2,000 calories a day is used for general nutrition advice.

DIRECTIONS

Combine all ingredients in a bowl. Refrigerate approximately 1 hour prior to serving.

Chicken Stew

Prep Time: 15 Cook Time: 60 Recipe quantity:

INGREDIENTS

- ½ cup water
- 1½ cups (~8oz) skinless chicken breast
- 1 tbsp olive oil
- ½ cup (2oz) carrot, grated or shredded
- 1 medium onion (8oz), diced
- 1 tsp garlic powder
- 1 cup frozen peas
- 4 cups sodium-free chicken broth
- 5 red potatoes, roughly chopped
- 1 tbsp dried parsley
- 1 tsp black pepper
- 1 tbsp cornstarch
- 2 tbsp water

Nutrition Facts	
Serving size	
Amount Per Serving	
Calories	**980**
	% Daily Value*
Total Fat 23g	**29%**
Saturated Fat 4g	**20%**
Trans Fat 0g	
Cholesterol 120mg	**40%**
Sodium 135mg	**6%**
Total Carbohydrate 108g	**39%**
Dietary Fiber 13g	**46%**
Total Sugars 20g	
Includes 4g Added Sugars	**8%**
Protein 75g	**150%**
Vitamin D 0mcg	0%
Calcium 162mg	10%
Iron 11mg	60%
Potassium 4476mg	100%

*The % Daily Value (DV) tells you how much a nutrient in a serving of food contributes to a daily diet. 2,000 calories a day is used for general nutrition advice.

DIRECTIONS

In a small skillet, add the ½ cup of water and then cook the breasts five minutes on each side or until thoroughly cooked. Meanwhile, add the oil to a soup pot over medium heat. Cook the carrots and onion until the onions are clear, approximately 5-7 minutes. Add the garlic, peas, and chicken broth and bring to a boil. Reduce heat to a simmer and then add the remaining ingredients through the black pepper. Simmer uncovered over medium-low heat for an additional 30 minutes. When the chicken has finished cooking, shred and then add to the soup pot. With five minutes of cook time remaining, mix the corn starch and water in a small bowl and then stir the mixture into the stew.

Chicken Stir Fry

Prep Time: 15 Cook Time: 20 Recipe quantity:

INGREDIENTS

Stir Fry Sauce

- 1 tbsp cornstarch
- 2 tbsp water
- ¼ cup sodium-free chicken broth
- 3 tbsp low sodium soy sauce
- ¼ cup honey
- 1 tbsp sesame oil
- ½ tsp crushed red pepper flakes

Filling

- 2 tbsp olive oil, divided
- 2 cups (10oz) chicken breast, cut into strips
- 2 cups (5oz) broccoli florets
- 1 cup (6oz) yellow bell pepper, cut into strips
- 1 cup (6oz) red bell pepper, cut into strips
- ½ cup (2oz) carrots, sliced
- 2 cups (5oz) cauliflower florets
- 2 tsp dried ginger
- ½ tsp garlic powder

Nutrition Facts

Serving size	
Amount Per Serving	
Calories	**1450**
	% Daily Value*
Total Fat 50g	**64%**
Saturated Fat 9g	**45%**
Trans Fat 0g	
Cholesterol 160mg	**53%**
Sodium 370mg	**16%**
Total Carbohydrate 155g	**56%**
Dietary Fiber 15g	**54%**
Total Sugars 125g	
Includes 0g Added Sugars	**0%**
Protein 88g	**176%**
Vitamin D 0mcg	0%
Calcium 155mg	10%
Iron 8mg	45%
Potassium 2542mg	50%

*The % Daily Value (DV) tells you how much a nutrient in a serving of food contributes to a daily diet. 2,000 calories a day is used for general nutrition advice.

DIRECTIONS

Prepare the sauce first. In a medium size bowl, whisk together the cornstarch and water. Then, add the remaining sauce ingredients, whisk to combine, and set aside. In a wide skillet or wok. heat 1 tbsp olive oil over medium-high heat then add the chicken and cook for 5 to 7 minutes or until cooked through, stirring often. Remove the chicken from the skillet, reduce the heat to medium and add the remaining tbsp of oil. Add the broccoli, bell pepper, carrots, and cauliflower and cook until slightly tender (~5-7 minutes), stirring often. Sprinkle on the ginger and garlic powder, stir to combine, and cook for an additional minute. Add the chicken back to the skillet and stir to combine, then add the prepared stir fry sauce and mix to incorporate. Bring to a boil, stirring occasionally, then simmer uncovered for 2-3 minutes before serving.

Chicken Tetrazzini

Prep Time: 15 Cook Time: 25 Recipe quantity:

INGREDIENTS

- **3 tbsp unsalted butter, divided**
- **2 cups skinless chicken breast, cut into 3/4" cubes**
- **1 cup (3oz) mushrooms, sliced**
- **¼ cup all-purpose flour**
- **½ tsp garlic powder**
- **3 cups sodium-free chicken broth**
- **½ cup milk**
- **½ cup heavy cream**
- **12 oz spaghetti, broken in half**
- **½ cup (2oz) frozen peas**
- **½ tsp black pepper**
- **3 tbsp Parmesan cheese**

Nutrition Facts

Serving size	
Amount Per Serving	
Calories	**2650**
	% Daily Value*
Total Fat 95g	**122%**
Saturated Fat 48g	**240%**
Trans Fat 0g	
Cholesterol 360mg	**120%**
Sodium 430mg	**19%**
Total Carbohydrate 314g	**114%**
Dietary Fiber 29g	**104%**
Total Sugars 27g	
Includes 3g Added Sugars	**6%**
Protein 121g	**242%**
Vitamin D 1mcg	4%
Calcium 475mg	35%
Iron 18mg	100%
Potassium 2655mg	60%

*The % Daily Value (DV) tells you how much a nutrient in a serving of food contributes to a daily diet. 2,000 calories a day is used for general nutrition advice.

DIRECTIONS

In a soup pot or Dutch oven, heat 1 tbsp butter over medium heat and add the chicken and mushrooms. Cook until the chicken has cooked through, approximately 8-10 minutes, then remove from the pot. Melt the remaining 2 tbsp butter then whisk in the flour. Once incorporated, add the garlic powder, chicken broth, milk, and heavy cream. Bring to a boil, then reduce the heat to a simmer. Add the spaghetti along with the cooked chicken and mushrooms. Simmer covered for 10-12 minutes or until the pasta has softened, stirring occasionally. Stir in the frozen peas and black pepper and allow to simmer for 8-10 minutes uncovered, stirring occasionally, or until the sauce has thickened adequately. Sprinkle the Parmesan over the top then toss to incorporate. Serve immediately.

Chili

Prep Time: 15 Cook Time: 150 Recipe quantity:

INGREDIENTS

- **2lbs ground beef (I prefer 80:20 ground chuck)**
- **2 (8oz) cans no-salt-added tomato sauce**
- **1 (14.5oz) can no-salt-added diced tomatoes, puréed**
- **1 (15oz) can no-salt-added kidney beans (drained)**
- **1 medium yellow onion (8oz), diced**
- **½ cup bell pepper (3oz), diced**
- **1/3 cup (1.5oz) celery, diced**
- **2 tsp cumin**
- **2 tbsp sodium-free chili powder**
- **1 tsp black pepper**
- **4 cups sodium-free chicken broth**

Nutrition Facts

Serving size	
Amount Per Serving	
Calories	**3030**
	% Daily Value*
Total Fat 176g	**226%**
Saturated Fat 72g	**360%**
Trans Fat 0g	
Cholesterol 640mg	**213%**
Sodium 810mg	**35%**
Total Carbohydrate 129g	**47%**
Dietary Fiber 43g	**154%**
Total Sugars 42g	
Includes 0g Added Sugars	**0%**
Protein 195g	**390%**
Vitamin D 0mcg	0%
Calcium 334mg	25%
Iron 33mg	180%
Potassium 7365mg	160%

*The % Daily Value (DV) tells you how much a nutrient in a serving of food contributes to a daily diet. 2,000 calories a day is used for general nutrition advice.

DIRECTIONS

Brown the ground beef over medium-high heat in a soup pot or Dutch oven. Drain, and then add all remaining ingredients to the pot. Bring to a boil, then cover and simmer for two hours, stirring occasionally.

Chili #2

Prep Time: 15 Cook Time: 120 Recipe quantity:

INGREDIENTS

- **2lbs ground beef (I prefer 80:20 ground chuck)**
- **3 (8oz) cans no-salt-added tomato sauce**
- **1 (15oz) can no-salt-added kidney beans, drained**
- **1 (15oz) can no-salt-added pinto beans, drained**
- **2 (14.5oz) can no-salt-added diced tomatoes, puréed**
- **1 medium yellow onion (8oz), diced**
- **2/3 cup (~3 oz) celery, diced**
- **1 cup (6oz) green bell pepper, diced**
- **1 tbsp cumin**
- **1 tbsp Worcestershire sauce**
- **3 tbsp sodium-free chili powder**
- **1 tsp black pepper**
- **1 cup water**
- **1 tbsp granulated sugar**

Nutrition Facts

Serving size	
Amount Per Serving	
Calories	**3560**
	% Daily Value*
Total Fat 176g	**226%**
Saturated Fat 72g	**360%**
Trans Fat 0g	
Cholesterol 640mg	**213%**
Sodium 1160mg	**50%**
Total Carbohydrate 227g	**83%**
Dietary Fiber 80g	**286%**
Total Sugars 70g	
Includes 0g Added Sugars	**0%**
Protein 224g	**448%**
Vitamin D 0mcg	0%
Calcium 521mg	40%
Iron 40mg	220%
Potassium 8672mg	180%

*The % Daily Value (DV) tells you how much a nutrient in a serving of food contributes to a daily diet. 2,000 calories a day is used for general nutrition advice.

DIRECTIONS

Brown the ground beef over medium-high heat in a soup pot or Dutch oven. Once browned, drain and then add the remaining ingredients. Bring to a boil, then simmer covered for 2 hours, stirring occasionally. Top with cheddar cheese or low-sodium crackers if desired.

Corn Chowder

Prep Time: 10 Cook Time: 40 Recipe quantity:

INGREDIENTS

- **4 slices low-sodium bacon, diced**
- **1 medium yellow onion (8oz), diced**
- **4 cups sodium-free chicken broth**
- **1 (15oz) can, no-salt-added sweet corn**
- **½ tsp garlic powder**
- **1 tsp dried thyme**
- **3 medium red potatoes, diced**
- **½ tsp black pepper**
- **1 cup heavy whipping cream**

Nutrition Facts	
Serving size	
Amount Per Serving	
Calories	1270
	% Daily Value*
Total Fat 94g	**121%**
Saturated Fat 64g	**320%**
Trans Fat 0g	
Cholesterol 360mg	**120%**
Sodium 740mg	**32%**
Total Carbohydrate 70g	**25%**
Dietary Fiber 6g	**21%**
Total Sugars 32g	
Includes 0g Added Sugars	**0%**
Protein 36g	**72%**
Vitamin D 16mcg	80%
Calcium 334mg	25%
Iron 7mg	40%
Potassium 2691mg	60%

*The % Daily Value (DV) tells you how much a nutrient in a serving of food contributes to a daily diet. 2,000 calories a day is used for general nutrition advice.

DIRECTIONS

In a soup pan, cook the bacon with the onion over medium heat until just prior to the bacon turning crispy (~7-8 minutes), then drain. Add the onion, chicken broth, corn, garlic powder, thyme, potatoes, and black pepper. Bring to a boil, then reduce the heat to simmer and cook for 30 minutes. Stir in the whipping cream and cook for 5 minutes, then serve.

Cottage Pie

Prep Time: 40 Cook Time: 30 Recipe quantity:

INGREDIENTS

- *4 cups mashed potatoes (see Mashed Potato recipe)
- 1½lbs ground beef (I prefer 80:20 ground chuck)
- 1 medium yellow onion (8oz), chopped
- ½ cup (2oz) carrots, grated or shredded
- 2/3 cup (~3oz) celery, chopped
- 1 cup (4oz) frozen peas
- 1 (15oz) can no-salt-added sweet corn
- 3 tbsp no-salt-added tomato paste
- 2 tbsp all-purpose flour
- 2 tsp Worcestershire sauce
- 1 tsp garlic powder
- 1 tsp dried rosemary
- 1 tsp dried thyme
- 1 tbsp dried parsley
- 2 cups sodium-free beef broth
- 1½ cups shredded cheddar cheese

Nutrition Facts	
Serving size	
Amount Per Serving	
Calories	4130
	% Daily Value*
Total Fat 258g	**331%**
Saturated Fat 127g	**635%**
Trans Fat 0g	
Cholesterol 850mg	**283%**
Sodium 2080mg	**90%**
Total Carbohydrate 251g	**91%**
Dietary Fiber 30g	**107%**
Total Sugars 55g	
Includes 0g Added Sugars	**0%**
Protein 205g	**410%**
Vitamin D 2mcg	10%
Calcium 2113mg	160%
Iron 32mg	180%
Potassium 8542mg	180%

*The % Daily Value (DV) tells you how much a nutrient in a serving of food contributes to a daily diet. 2,000 calories a day is used for general nutrition advice.

DIRECTIONS

Prepare the mashed potatoes using the mashed potato recipe from this book. For best results the mashed potatoes should be warm when assembling the Cottage Pie. Meanwhile, brown the ground beef along with the onion, carrots, and celery. When browned, drain the liquid then add the frozen peas, corn, tomato paste, and flour. Stir and cook for 1 minute, then add the remaining ingredients except for the cheddar cheese and mashed potatoes, and stir to mix. Bring to a boil then simmer uncovered for 10 minutes to allow the sauce to thicken. Preheat the oven to 375°F. Assemble the pie by first spreading the meat mix in a 9"x13" baking dish, then top with the mashed potatoes. Sprinkle the cheddar cheese over the top and then bake in the oven for 25 minutes. Allow to rest for 10 minutes prior to serving.

Creamy Pasta

Prep Time: 15 Cook Time: 15 Recipe quantity:

INGREDIENTS

- **16 oz rotini, penne, or bowtie pasta**
- **1 tbsp olive oil**
- **½ medium yellow onion (4oz), diced**
- **½ tsp garlic powder**
- **½ tsp black pepper**
- **2 (15oz) cans no-salt-added diced tomatoes, drained**
- **½ cup heavy whipping cream**
- **1 tbsp dried basil**

Nutrition Facts	
Serving size	
Amount Per Serving	
Calories	2340
	% Daily Value*
Total Fat 62g	**79%**
Saturated Fat 30g	**150%**
Trans Fat 0g	
Cholesterol 160mg	**53%**
Sodium 150mg	**7%**
Total Carbohydrate 378g	**137%**
Dietary Fiber 32g	**114%**
Total Sugars 39g	
Includes 0g Added Sugars	**0%**
Protein 64g	**128%**
Vitamin D 0mcg	0%
Calcium 206mg	15%
Iron 19mg	110%
Potassium 2781mg	60%

*The % Daily Value (DV) tells you how much a nutrient in a serving of food contributes to a daily diet. 2,000 calories a day is used for general nutrition advice.

DIRECTIONS

Cook the pasta according to package directions, then drain. In a large skillet, heat the olive oil and then cook the onion until translucent (~5-7 minutes). Add the garlic powder, black pepper, and diced tomatoes and cook for 2-3 minutes, stirring constantly. Add the cream, then stir to combine. Heat to boiling, then reduce the heat and simmer for 5 minutes. Then, add the cooked pasta and basil and stir to incorporate. Serve immediately.

Creamy Pork Chops

Prep Time: 10 Cook Time: 25 Recipe quantity:

INGREDIENTS

- **2 tbsp olive oil**
- **3 pork chops**
- **2 tbsp unsalted butter**
- **½ medium yellow onion (4oz), diced**
- **1½ cups (~5oz) sliced mushrooms**
- **3 slices low-sodium bacon, diced**
- **1 cup sodium-free beef broth**
- **½ tsp garlic powder**
- **2 tsp dried parsley**
- **¾ cup heavy whipping cream**

Nutrition Facts	
Serving size	
Amount Per Serving	
Calories	**2120**
	% Daily Value*
Total Fat 136g	**174%**
Saturated Fat 63g	**315%**
Trans Fat 0g	
Cholesterol 765mg	**255%**
Sodium 810mg	**35%**
Total Carbohydrate 74g	**27%**
Dietary Fiber 5g	**18%**
Total Sugars 21g	
Includes 0g Added Sugars	**0%**
Protein 140g	**280%**
Vitamin D 17mcg	80%
Calcium 157mg	10%
Iron 7mg	40%
Potassium 3127mg	70%

*The % Daily Value (DV) tells you how much a nutrient in a serving of food contributes to a daily diet. 2,000 calories a day is used for general nutrition advice.

DIRECTIONS

In a wide skillet, heat the olive oil over medium heat and then add the pork chops. Cook on each side approximately 4 minutes or until cooked through. Remove the pork chops and wipe out the pan. Melt the butter and add the onion and mushrooms. Cook for 1 minute, then add the bacon and cook until just before the bacon gets crispy, approximately 7-8 minutes. Add the remaining ingredients up to the parsley and stir to incorporate. Bring to a boil, then reduce the heat to medium. Add the heavy cream and pork chops, pushing each into the sauce. Simmer for 10 minutes uncovered. Remove from the heat and allow to rest 5 minutes before serving.

Fajitas

Prep Time: 20 Cook Time: 20 Recipe quantity:

INGREDIENTS

- ½ tsp black pepper
- ½ tsp cumin
- 2 tsp sodium-free chili powder
- ½ tsp garlic powder
- ⅛ tsp sodium-free cayenne pepper
- 2 tbsp olive oil + 1 tbsp
- 1 tbsp lime juice
- 1lb sirloin, cut into 1" x ½" strips
- 1 large yellow onion (12oz), cut into ¼" wide strips
- 1 red bell pepper, cut into ¼" wide strips
- 1 green bell pepper, cut into ¼" wide strips
- 1 cup shredded cheddar
- 10 corn tortillas

Nutrition Facts	
Serving size	
Amount Per Serving	
Calories	**1880**
	% Daily Value*
Total Fat 116g	**149%**
Saturated Fat 42g	**210%**
Trans Fat 0g	
Cholesterol 400mg	**133%**
Sodium 1070mg	**47%**
Total Carbohydrate 145g	**53%**
Dietary Fiber 20g	**71%**
Total Sugars 14g	
Includes 0g Added Sugars	**0%**
Protein 185g	**370%**
Vitamin D 0mcg	0%
Calcium 1047mg	80%
Iron 14mg	80%
Potassium 1121mg	25%

*The % Daily Value (DV) tells you how much a nutrient in a serving of food contributes to a daily diet. 2,000 calories a day is used for general nutrition advice.

DIRECTIONS

Mix together the black pepper, cumin, chili powder, garlic powder, and cayenne pepper. Reserve ½ tsp of this mixed dry spice, then in a small bowl mix the remaining dry spices with the 2tbsp olive oil and the lime juice. Place the sirloin strips into a sandwich bag and add the wet spice mixture. Work the mixture into the strips, then set aside while you prepare the remaining filling. In a medium-sized skillet over medium-high heat, add the remaining 1 tbsp olive oil. Cook the onion and peppers until they begin to soften, approximately 5-7 minutes, then transfer to a plate. Add the seasoned sirloin to the skillet and, stirring often, cook until no pink remains (~7-10 minutes). Add the onions and peppers back to the skillet, sprinkle on the reserved spice mix, then cook for 1 minute. To serve, spoon ¼ cup fajita mix onto a warmed corn tortilla, then top with a sprinkle of cheddar cheese. Feel free to add sour cream, guacamole, or your favorite salsa for even more flavor.

Fettuccine Alfredo

Prep Time: 10 Cook Time: 15 Recipe quantity:

INGREDIENTS

- 1lb fettuccine noodles
- 2 tbsp unsalted butter
- 1 tsp garlic powder
- 3 cups heavy whipping cream
- ¾ cup Parmesan cheese
- ½ tsp black pepper

Nutrition Facts

Serving size	
Amount Per Serving	
Calories	**4510**
	% Daily Value*
Total Fat 288g	**369%**
Saturated Fat 188g	**940%**
Trans Fat 0g	
Cholesterol 1050mg	**350%**
Sodium 1140mg	**50%**
Total Carbohydrate 387g	**141%**
Dietary Fiber 24g	**86%**
Total Sugars 56g	
Includes 0g Added Sugars	**0%**
Protein 81g	**162%**
Vitamin D 0mcg	0%
Calcium 1185mg	90%
Iron 19mg	110%
Potassium 1914mg	40%

*The % Daily Value (DV) tells you how much a nutrient in a serving of food contributes to a daily diet. 2,000 calories a day is used for general nutrition advice.

DIRECTIONS

Cook the noodles according to package directions, then drain. While cooking, make the Alfredo sauce in a medium skillet by first melting the butter then adding the garlic powder and whipping cream. Bring to a boil, then reduce to simmer and add the Parmesan cheese and black pepper. Once incorporated, add the cooked fettucine noodles and mix with the sauce.

Fried Chicken

Prep Time: 20 Cook Time: 30 Recipe quantity:

INGREDIENTS

- **3lbs chicken drumsticks, skinless**
- **4 cups all-purpose flour, divided into 1 cup and 3 cups**
- **1 tbsp garlic powder**
- **1 tbsp sodium-free chili powder**
- **1 tsp cumin**
- **1 tsp dried parsley**
- **1 tbsp course ground black pepper**
- **3 eggs**
- **¼ cup milk**
- **4 cups vegetable or canola oil for frying**

Nutrition Facts

Serving size	
Amount Per Serving	
Calories	**2670**
	% Daily Value*
Total Fat 70g	**90%**
Saturated Fat 16g	**80%**
Trans Fat 0g	
Cholesterol 860mg	**287%**
Sodium 410mg	**18%**
Total Carbohydrate 189g	**69%**
Dietary Fiber 24g	**86%**
Total Sugars 3g	
Includes 0g Added Sugars	**0%**
Protein 251g	**502%**
Vitamin D 3mcg	15%
Calcium 211mg	15%
Iron 30mg	170%
Potassium 3383mg	70%

*The % Daily Value (DV) tells you how much a nutrient in a serving of food contributes to a daily diet. 2,000 calories a day is used for general nutrition advice.

DIRECTIONS

Set up three medium-sized bowls on the counter. In one bowl, add 1 cup of flour along with the garlic powder, chili powder, cumin, parsley, and black pepper. Stir to combine. In a separate bowl, beat the eggs with the milk. In a third bowl, add the remaining flour. Heat the frying oil to 350°F in a wide skillet. Meanwhile, remove the skin from the drumstick if desired, and then dredge thoroughly in the first bowl, shaking off any extra coating. Next, dip the drumstick in the egg wash, allowing any excess to drip off. Finally, dredge thoroughly in the final flour bowl and shake off any excess flour. Carefully place the drumstick in the heated oil, cooking on each side approximately 8-10 minutes or until the internal temperature reaches 165°F. Once done frying, remove the drumsticks to a drying rack and allow to rest for five minutes before serving.

Garden Pasta

Prep Time: 10 Cook Time: 15 Recipe quantity:

INGREDIENTS

- **16 ounces pasta (I prefer spaghetti, rotini, or penne)**
- **2 cups (10oz) cherry or grape tomatoes, quartered**
- **1½ cups shredded mozzarella cheese**
- **1 tsp garlic powder**
- **1 tbsp dried basil**
- **½ tsp black pepper**
- **3 tbsp olive oil**

Nutrition Facts	
Serving size	
Amount Per Serving	
Calories	2510
	% Daily Value*
Total Fat 86g	**110%**
Saturated Fat 24g	**120%**
Trans Fat 0g	
Cholesterol 120mg	**40%**
Sodium 1160mg	**50%**
Total Carbohydrate 363g	**132%**
Dietary Fiber 33g	**118%**
Total Sugars 16g	
Includes 0g Added Sugars	**0%**
Protein 102g	**204%**
Vitamin D 0mcg	0%
Calcium 1347mg	100%
Iron 19mg	110%
Potassium 1984mg	40%

*The % Daily Value (DV) tells you how much a nutrient in a serving of food contributes to a daily diet. 2,000 calories a day is used for general nutrition advice.

DIRECTIONS

In a saucepan, cook the pasta according to manufacturer directions. While cooking, in a separate bowl, combine the tomatoes, mozzarella cheese, garlic powder, dried basil, and black pepper. Drain the pasta and return to the same pot. Toss the pasta with the olive oil, then add the mixed ingredients from the bowl. Serve immediately.

Garlic Pasta

Prep Time: 5 Cook Time: 15 Recipe quantity:

INGREDIENTS

- **12 oz pasta (I prefer spaghetti or rotini)**
- **3 tbsp olive oil**
- **1 tsp garlic powder**
- **1 tbsp dried basil**

Nutrition Facts	
Serving size	
Amount Per Serving	
Calories	**1570**
	% Daily Value*
Total Fat 48g	**62%**
Saturated Fat 6g	**30%**
Trans Fat 0g	
Cholesterol 0mg	**0%**
Sodium 0mg	**0%**
Total Carbohydrate 254g	**92%**
Dietary Fiber 18g	**64%**
Total Sugars 6g	
Includes 0g Added Sugars	**0%**
Protein 43g	**86%**
Vitamin D 0mcg	0%
Calcium 87mg	6%
Iron 13mg	70%
Potassium 718mg	15%

*The % Daily Value (DV) tells you how much a nutrient in a serving of food contributes to a daily diet. 2,000 calories a day is used for general nutrition advice.

DIRECTIONS

In a saucepan, cook the pasta according to manufacturer directions. When done cooking, drain and return to the same pot. Drizzle the olive oil over the pasta and toss to coat evenly. Sprinkle the garlic powder and basil over the pasta, then toss to coat. Serve immediately.

Goulash

Prep Time: 15 Cook Time: 20 Recipe quantity:

INGREDIENTS

- 1lb ground beef (I prefer 80:20 ground chuck)
- ½ medium yellow onion (4oz), diced
- 1 cup bell pepper (~6oz), diced
- 1 tsp garlic powder
- 1 cup water
- 2 (8oz) cans no-salt-added tomato sauce
- 2 (14.5oz) cans no-salt-added diced tomatoes
- 2 tbsp Worcestershire sauce
- 1 tsp dried oregano
- 1 tsp dried basil
- 16oz pasta noodles (I prefer rotini, bowtie, or elbow)

Nutrition Facts	
Serving size	
Amount Per Serving	
Calories	3130
	% Daily Value*
Total Fat 96g	**123%**
Saturated Fat 36g	**180%**
Trans Fat 0g	
Cholesterol 320mg	**107%**
Sodium 840mg	**37%**
Total Carbohydrate 408g	**148%**
Dietary Fiber 41g	**146%**
Total Sugars 57g	
Includes 0g Added Sugars	**0%**
Protein 150g	**300%**
Vitamin D 0mcg	0%
Calcium 186mg	15%
Iron 27mg	150%
Potassium 4805mg	100%

*The % Daily Value (DV) tells you how much a nutrient in a serving of food contributes to a daily diet. 2,000 calories a day is used for general nutrition advice.

DIRECTIONS

In a wide skillet, brown the ground beef over medium-high heat along with the onion and bell pepper. Drain the liquid, then add the remaining ingredients except the pasta, stirring to mix well. Bring to a boil then reduce to a simmer, covered, for 15 minutes. While simmering, in a separate pot prepare the pasta noodles according to package directions, then drain. Add the cooked pasta noodles to the beef mixture, stir to combine, then simmer for five additional minutes, stirring occasionally.

Goulash #2

Prep Time: 25 Cook Time: 25 Recipe quantity:

INGREDIENTS

- 1lb ground beef (I prefer 80:20 ground chuck)
- ½ yellow onion (4oz), diced
- ½ cup (~3oz) green or red bell pepper, diced
- 1 (14.5oz) can no-salt-added diced tomatoes
- 2 tbsp no-salt-added tomato paste
- 1 (8oz) can no-salt-added tomato sauce
- 1 tbsp Italian seasoning
- 1 tsp garlic powder
- 1 tsp black pepper
- 1 tbsp Worcestershire sauce
- 16oz elbow noodles

Nutrition Facts

Serving size	
Amount Per Serving	
Calories	**3010**
	% Daily Value*
Total Fat 96g	**123%**
Saturated Fat 36g	**180%**
Trans Fat 0g	
Cholesterol 320mg	**107%**
Sodium 620mg	**27%**
Total Carbohydrate 388g	**141%**
Dietary Fiber 35g	**125%**
Total Sugars 42g	
Includes 0g Added Sugars	**0%**
Protein 144g	**288%**
Vitamin D 0mcg	0%
Calcium 219mg	15%
Iron 33mg	180%
Potassium 4167mg	90%

*The % Daily Value (DV) tells you how much a nutrient in a serving of food contributes to a daily diet. 2,000 calories a day is used for general nutrition advice.

DIRECTIONS

In a medium saucepan, brown the ground beef over medium-high heat along with the diced onion and pepper, then drain. Add the remaining ingredients through the Worcestershire sauce. Heat to boiling, then simmer uncovered for 20 minutes or until the mixture thickens. While simmering, in a soup pot cook the elbow noodles according to manufacturer directions. Drain the noodles. then place them back in the soup pot. Add the meat sauce to the pot then stir to combine. Top each bowl with some Parmesan cheese, if desired.

Green Beans and Beef Over Rice

Prep Time: 10 Cook Time: 15 Recipe quantity:

INGREDIENTS

- **1lb ground beef (I prefer 80:20 ground chuck)**
- **½ medium yellow onion (4oz), diced**
- **1½ cups water + ¼ cup water**
- **½ tsp garlic powder**
- **3 tbsp low sodium soy sauce**
- **1 tbsp dark molasses**
- **1 (15oz) can no-salt-added French style green beans, drained and chopped**
- **1 tbsp cornstarch**
- **2 cups instant rice**

Nutrition Facts

Serving size	
Amount Per Serving	
Calories	**2170**
	% Daily Value*
Total Fat 88g	**113%**
Saturated Fat 36g	**180%**
Trans Fat 0g	
Cholesterol 320mg	**107%**
Sodium 560mg	**24%**
Total Carbohydrate 232g	**84%**
Dietary Fiber 5g	**18%**
Total Sugars 65g	
Includes 0g Added Sugars	**0%**
Protein 104g	**208%**
Vitamin D 0mcg	0%
Calcium 324mg	25%
Iron 18mg	100%
Potassium 1889mg	40%

*The % Daily Value (DV) tells you how much a nutrient in a serving of food contributes to a daily diet. 2,000 calories a day is used for general nutrition advice.

DIRECTIONS

Prepare the instant rice according to package directions. Meanwhile, in a skillet, brown the ground beef over medium-high heat along with the chopped onion. Once browned, add the 1 ½ cups water, garlic powder, soy sauce, molasses, and green beans, and stir to combine. Heat to boiling, then reduce to a simmer and cook uncovered for 10 minutes. Meanwhile, in a small bowl mix the cornstarch with the ¼ cup water and stir to dissolve. With about two minutes remaining in the cook time, add the corn starch mixture to the skillet and stir to combine. Simmer an additional 2-3 minutes or until thickened. Serve over the prepared rice.

Ground Beef Ramen

Prep Time: 10 Cook Time: 10 Recipe quantity: ———

INGREDIENTS

- 1lb ground beef (I prefer 80:20 ground chuck)
- ½ medium yellow onion (4oz), diced
- ¼ cup (1oz) carrot, grated or shredded
- 1 cup (4oz) frozen peas
- 1 tsp black pepper
- 2 sodium-free chicken bouillon packets (1 packet = 1 cup broth)
- 2 packages ramen noodles, shredded (discard the seasoning packet)

Nutrition Facts

Nutrition Facts	
Serving size	
Amount Per Serving	
Calories	**2050**
	% Daily Value*
Total Fat 116g	**149%**
Saturated Fat 50g	**250%**
Trans Fat 0g	
Cholesterol 320mg	**107%**
Sodium 780mg	**34%**
Total Carbohydrate 134g	**49%**
Dietary Fiber 12g	**43%**
Total Sugars 12g	
Includes 2g Added Sugars	**4%**
Protein 107g	**214%**
Vitamin D 0mcg	0%
Calcium 90mg	6%
Iron 16mg	90%
Potassium 2377mg	50%

*The % Daily Value (DV) tells you how much a nutrient in a serving of food contributes to a daily diet. 2,000 calories a day is used for general nutrition advice.

DIRECTIONS

Brown the ground beef along with the diced onion and carrot, discarding the liquid once complete. Add the frozen peas and black pepper, then sprinkle the bouillon packet contents over the meat mixture. Stir to incorporate, then cook uncovered over medium-high heat for 3-4 minutes or until the peas have cooked through. In a small saucepan, boil 3-4 cups of water. Once boiling, add the shredded ramen noodles and cook for approximately 2 minutes, or until the noodles have cooked and softened, then drain. Add the noodles to the ground beef mixture, stir, and serve.

Hamburger Patties

Prep Time: 10 Cook Time: 10 Recipe quantity:

INGREDIENTS

- **1lb ground beef (I prefer 80:20 ground chuck)**
- **4 slices low-sodium bacon, finely diced**
- **1 egg**
- **1 tsp onion powder**
- **¼ cup unseasoned breadcrumbs**
- **1 tbsp Worcestershire sauce**
- **1 tsp garlic powder**
- **½ tsp black pepper**
- **½ cup water**

Nutrition Facts	
Serving size	
Amount Per Serving	
Calories	1380
	% Daily Value*
Total Fat 100g	**128%**
Saturated Fat 42g	**210%**
Trans Fat 0g	
Cholesterol 525mg	**175%**
Sodium 870mg	**38%**
Total Carbohydrate 20g	**7%**
Dietary Fiber 1g	**4%**
Total Sugars 4g	
Includes 0g Added Sugars	**0%**
Protein 97g	**194%**
Vitamin D 1mcg	4%
Calcium 106mg	8%
Iron 16mg	90%
Potassium 1280mg	25%

*The % Daily Value (DV) tells you how much a nutrient in a serving of food contributes to a daily diet. 2,000 calories a day is used for general nutrition advice.

DIRECTIONS

In a wide skillet, cook the bacon over medium-high heat to just prior to crispy. Once cooked, drain and move the bacon to a paper towel to dry. In a mixing bowl, combine all ingredients including the bacon. The mixture should be mushy but not dry - if it is dry, add incremental small amounts of water until it is slightly mushy. Form patties of desired thickness and size, then in the same skillet used for the bacon, discard any remaining grease and cook patties uncovered over medium heat for 5-6 minutes per side or until the patty's internal temperature reaches at least 160°F.

Lasagna

Prep Time: 20 Cook Time: 45 Recipe quantity:

INGREDIENTS

- 1lb ground beef (I prefer 80:20 ground chuck)
- 1 medium yellow onion (8oz), diced
- 1 medium bell pepper, diced
- 1 tsp garlic powder
- 3 (8oz) cans no-salt-added tomato sauce
- 2 tbsp no-salt-added tomato paste
- 1 (14.5oz) can no-salt-added diced tomatoes
- 2 tsp dried oregano
- 1 tbsp dried parsley
- 1 tbsp dried basil
- 1 tbsp red wine vinegar
- 1 tbsp sugar
- 10 oz oven-ready lasagna noodles
- 2 cups ricotta cheese
- 1 cup shredded Mozzarella cheese + 1/4 cup
- ¼ cup Parmesan cheese

Nutrition Facts	
Serving size	
Amount Per Serving	
Calories	**4060**
	% Daily Value*
Total Fat 207g	**265%**
Saturated Fat 97g	**485%**
Trans Fat 0g	
Cholesterol 720mg	**240%**
Sodium 2190mg	**95%**
Total Carbohydrate 328g	**119%**
Dietary Fiber 34g	**121%**
Total Sugars 63g	
Includes 0g Added Sugars	**0%**
Protein 214g	**428%**
Vitamin D 0mcg	0%
Calcium 2580mg	200%
Iron 24mg	130%
Potassium 6040mg	130%

*The % Daily Value (DV) tells you how much a nutrient in a serving of food contributes to a daily diet. 2,000 calories a day is used for general nutrition advice.

DIRECTIONS

In a large skillet, brown the ground beef along over medium-high heat along with the diced onion and bell pepper, then drain. Add the remaining ingredients through the 1 tbsp of sugar. Heat to boiling, then simmer uncovered for 20 minutes or until the mixture thickens. Preheat the oven to 350°F. Spray a 9"x13" baking dish with cooking spray. Then, assemble the lasagna by adding ¼ of the meat sauce on the bottom, followed by a single layer of oven-ready noodles, 1 cup of Ricotta cheese, and ½ cup of Mozzarella cheese. Repeat for a second layer, then finish with a layer of meat, noodles, and meat. Top with the ¼ cup of Mozzarella cheese. To prevent from drying out, cover tightly with aluminum foil, then bake for 50-60 minutes or until bubbling. When complete, remove from the oven, uncover, and allow the lasagna to rest for 10 minutes.

Lemon Pepper Chicken

Prep Time: 15 Cook Time: 45 Recipe quantity:

INGREDIENTS

- 3 cups (15oz) skinless chicken breast
- 1 tbsp no-salt lemon pepper seasoning
- ¼ cup olive oil
- 2 tsp dried basil
- 2 tsp dried oregano
- ¼ cup lemon juice
- 3 cups instant rice

Nutrition Facts	
Serving size	
Amount Per Serving	
Calories	2150
	% Daily Value*
Total Fat 71g	91%
Saturated Fat 12g	60%
Trans Fat 0g	
Cholesterol 240mg	80%
Sodium 150mg	7%
Total Carbohydrate 220g	80%
Dietary Fiber 0g	0%
Total Sugars 0g	
Includes 0g Added Sugars	0%
Protein 129g	258%
Vitamin D 0mcg	0%
Calcium 38mg	2%
Iron 9mg	50%
Potassium 1260mg	25%

*The % Daily Value (DV) tells you how much a nutrient in a serving of food contributes to a daily diet. 2,000 calories a day is used for general nutrition advice.

DIRECTIONS

Preheat the oven to 350°F. Spray a 9"x13" baking dish with the cooking spray. Mix the lemon pepper, olive oil, basil, and oregano in a small bowl. Rub the olive oil mixture over each chicken breast, then lay the chicken breasts in the baking dish. Drizzle each with the lemon juice. Bake for 45 minutes in the oven or until the internal temperature reaches 165°F. While baking, prepare the rice according to package directions. To serve, lay one breast over a pile of prepared rice and drizzle with juices from the baking dish.

Meatballs

Prep Time: 15 Cook Time: 35 Recipe quantity:

INGREDIENTS

- 1 tbsp olive oil
- 1 medium yellow onion (8oz), minced
- ½ tsp garlic powder
- 2lbs ground beef (I prefer 80:20 ground chuck)
- 2 eggs
- ½ cup Parmesan cheese
- 2 tbsp dried parsley
- 1 cup unseasoned breadcrumbs
- ½ cup water

Nutrition Facts

Serving size	
Amount Per Serving	
Calories	**2990**
	% Daily Value*
Total Fat 212g	**272%**
Saturated Fat 86g	**430%**
Trans Fat 0g	
Cholesterol 1050mg	**350%**
Sodium 1420mg	**62%**
Total Carbohydrate 58g	**21%**
Dietary Fiber 3g	**11%**
Total Sugars 8g	
Includes 0g Added Sugars	**0%**
Protein 190g	**380%**
Vitamin D 2mcg	10%
Calcium 603mg	45%
Iron 24mg	130%
Potassium 2769mg	60%

*The % Daily Value (DV) tells you how much a nutrient in a serving of food contributes to a daily diet. 2,000 calories a day is used for general nutrition advice.

DIRECTIONS

Preheat the oven to 350°F. In a large oven-safe skillet, add the olive oil and onions and cook over medium heat until the onions become translucent (~5-7 minutes). Meanwhile, in a bowl add the remaining ingredients and mix thoroughly with your hands. Add the cooked onions and give one final mix. Then, form the mixture into individual 1.5" balls and add them to the skillet. Once all meatballs have been added to the skillet, brown each meatball on all sides (~8 minutes total), then transfer the skillet to the oven and cook for an additional 20-25 minutes or until the internal temperature of the meatballs reaches 160°F.

Meatloaf

Prep Time: 15 Cook Time: 75 Recipe quantity:

INGREDIENTS

- 1 tbsp olive oil
- 1 medium yellow onion (8oz), diced
- 1 cup unseasoned breadcrumbs
- 2 eggs
- 2lbs ground beef (I prefer 80:20 ground chuck)
- ½ cup milk
- 1 tsp ground black pepper
- 1 tbsp Worcestershire sauce
- 1 tbsp yellow mustard
- 1 tbsp no-salt-added tomato paste
- 1 tsp garlic powder

Topping

- ½ cup sodium-free ketchup
- 2 tsp brown sugar
- 1 tbsp Worcestershire sauce
- 1 tsp yellow mustard

Nutrition Facts

Serving size	
Amount Per Serving	
Calories	**3030**
	% Daily Value*
Total Fat 190g	**244%**
Saturated Fat 79g	**395%**
Trans Fat 0g	
Cholesterol 1030mg	**343%**
Sodium 1600mg	**70%**
Total Carbohydrate 123g	**45%**
Dietary Fiber 4g	**14%**
Total Sugars 70g	
Includes 32g Added Sugars	**64%**
Protein 179g	**358%**
Vitamin D 3mcg	15%
Calcium 341mg	25%
Iron 28mg	160%
Potassium 3879mg	80%

*The % Daily Value (DV) tells you how much a nutrient in a serving of food contributes to a daily diet. 2,000 calories a day is used for general nutrition advice.

DIRECTIONS

Preheat the oven to 375°F. In a small skillet, heat the olive oil and then add the diced onion. Cook until the onion starts to turn translucent (~5-7 minutes), then remove from the heat. In a large bowl, mix all non-topping ingredients together thoroughly, including the cooked onion. Spray a loaf pan with cooking spray and pour in the mixed ingredients. Bake for 75 minutes or until the internal temperature of the loaf reaches 160°F. Mix the topping ingredients, and with 10 minutes of cooking time left, pour the topping over the meatloaf, and then return the meatloaf to the oven. Allow to rest for 10 minutes prior to serving.

Mexican Casserole

Prep Time: 20 Cook Time: 30 Recipe quantity:

INGREDIENTS

- 1lb ground beef (I prefer 80:20 ground chuck)
- 1 medium yellow onion (8oz), diced
- 1 cup water
- 2 tbsp sodium-free chili powder
- ½ tsp garlic powder
- 1 tbsp dried parsley
- 1 cup no-salt-added sweet corn, drained
- 1 (15oz) can no-salt-added black beans, drained
- 2 (14.5oz) cans no-salt-added diced tomatoes, drained
- 10 yellow corn tortillas
- 1 cup sour cream
- 1 cup grated cheddar cheese

Nutrition Facts	
Serving size	
Amount Per Serving	
Calories	**3210**
	% Daily Value*
Total Fat 174g	**223%**
Saturated Fat 88g	**440%**
Trans Fat 0g	
Cholesterol 600mg	**200%**
Sodium 1360mg	**59%**
Total Carbohydrate 231g	**84%**
Dietary Fiber 40g	**143%**
Total Sugars 39g	
Includes 0g Added Sugars	**0%**
Protein 159g	**318%**
Vitamin D 0mcg	0%
Calcium 1487mg	110%
Iron 19mg	110%
Potassium 5324mg	110%

*The % Daily Value (DV) tells you how much a nutrient in a serving of food contributes to a daily diet. 2,000 calories a day is used for general nutrition advice.

DIRECTIONS

Brown the ground beef over medium-high heat along with the diced onion. After browned, add the water, chili powder, garlic powder, and parsley. Bring to a boil, then simmer uncovered for 7-8 minutes or until most of the water is gone. Add the corn, beans, and tomatoes. Mix well , bring to a boil, then simmer uncovered for 5 minutes. Meanwhile, spray 9" x 13" baking dish with cooking spray and preheat the oven to 350°F. Once the meat mixture is ready, place approximately 1 cup of the mixture on the bottom of the baking dish. Layer 5 of the tortillas on top of the ground beef mixture, followed by half of the sour cream. Spoon half of the remaining beef mixture on top of the first layer of tortillas and sour cream. Layer the rest of the corn tortillas and then the rest of the sour cream, followed by the remaining beef mixture. Top with the grated cheese. Bake for 30 minutes or until bubbling. Allow to stand for 5 minutes before serving.

Minestrone Soup

Prep Time: 15 Cook Time: 35 Recipe quantity:

INGREDIENTS

- 1lb ground beef (I prefer 80:20 ground chuck)
- 1 medium yellow onion (8oz), diced
- 4 oz dry pasta (I prefer ditalini or other short pasta)
- 4 cups sodium-free beef broth
- ½ cup (2oz) carrots, shredded or grated
- 1 (15oz) can no-salt-added sweet corn
- 1 (15oz) can no-salt-added green beans
- 1 (15oz) can no-salt-added kidney beans, drained
- 1 (15oz) can no-salt-added diced tomatoes, puréed
- 4 tbsp no-salt-added tomato paste
- 1 tbsp Italian seasoning
- ½ tsp dried thyme
- ½ tsp dried basil
- ½ tsp black pepper
- ½ tsp garlic powder

Nutrition Facts

Serving size	
Amount Per Serving	
Calories	**2430**
	% Daily Value*
Total Fat 90g	**115%**
Saturated Fat 36g	**180%**
Trans Fat 0g	
Cholesterol 320mg	**107%**
Sodium 680mg	**30%**
Total Carbohydrate 250g	**91%**
Dietary Fiber 54g	**193%**
Total Sugars 60g	
Includes 0g Added Sugars	**0%**
Protein 137g	**274%**
Vitamin D 0mcg	0%
Calcium 586mg	45%
Iron 28mg	160%
Potassium 7394mg	160%

*The % Daily Value (DV) tells you how much a nutrient in a serving of food contributes to a daily diet. 2,000 calories a day is used for general nutrition advice.

DIRECTIONS

In a soup pot, brown the ground beef over medium-high heat along with the onion, then drain. While browning, cook the pasta according to package directions, then drain and set aside. In the soup pot with the ground beef and onion, add the remaining ingredients, stir to combine, then bring to a boil. Simmer, covered, for 30 minutes. With 5 minutes left, add the cooked pasta and stir to combine.

Mongolian Beef Ramen

Prep Time: 20 Cook Time: 30 Recipe quantity:

INGREDIENTS

- 1lb stew meat, sirloin, or top steak, sliced into 1" by ½" strips
- 3 tbsp cornstarch
- 1 tbsp olive oil
- 1 tbsp sesame oil
- ½ tsp garlic powder
- 1 tsp ginger
- 2 tbsp brown sugar
- 2 tbsp low-sodium soy sauce
- ⅛ tsp red pepper flakes
- 1 cup sodium-free chicken broth
- 1 package ramen noodles, broken (discard flavor packets)
- 2 cups (5oz) broccoli florets
- ½ cup (1oz) carrot, grated
- ½ cup (2oz) diced green onions
- 1 tsp sesame seeds

Nutrition Facts	
Serving size	
Amount Per Serving	
Calories	**1480**
	% Daily Value*
Total Fat 70g	**90%**
Saturated Fat 23g	**115%**
Trans Fat 0g	
Cholesterol 280mg	**93%**
Sodium 750mg	**33%**
Total Carbohydrate 153g	**56%**
Dietary Fiber 13g	**46%**
Total Sugars 62g	
Includes 1g Added Sugars	**2%**
Protein 161g	**322%**
Vitamin D 0mcg	0%
Calcium 273mg	20%
Iron 16mg	90%
Potassium 1542mg	35%

*The % Daily Value (DV) tells you how much a nutrient in a serving of food contributes to a daily diet. 2,000 calories a day is used for general nutrition advice.

DIRECTIONS

In a large bag, toss the meat with the corn starch. Heat the olive oil over medium heat in a skillet and then add the meat, stirring often to brown all sides. Remove the meat and add the sesame oil, garlic powder, and ginger and cook for one minute, stirring constantly. Add the brown sugar, soy sauce, red pepper flakes, and chicken broth and bring to a boil then reduce the heat and simmer for five minutes or until the sauce thickens. While thickening, cook the ramen noodles in a separate saucepan according to package directions, then drain. Once the sauce has thickened, add the carrots, broccoli, and meat. Bring to a boil, then reduce to a simmer and cook covered for 10 minutes, stirring occasionally. Prior to serving, add the ramen noodles, green onions, and the sesame seeds to the skillet and stir to mix.

Nachos Grande

Prep Time: 15 Cook Time: 0 Recipe quantity:

INGREDIENTS

- 1lb ground beef (I prefer 80:20 ground chuck)
- 1 cup water
- 1 tbsp dried parsley
- 1 tbsp sodium-free chili powder
- ½ tsp garlic powder
- 1½ cups unsalted tortilla chips, crushed
- ¼ cup shredded cheddar cheese
- ½ medium yellow onion (4oz), diced
- 1 cup (~8oz) roma tomato, diced
- 2 cups iceberg lettuce, diced
- 2 tbsp sour cream

Nutrition Facts

Serving size

Amount Per Serving

Calories 1630

	% Daily Value*
Total Fat 114g	**146%**
Saturated Fat 47g	**235%**
Trans Fat 0g	
Cholesterol 370mg	**123%**
Sodium 530mg	**23%**
Total Carbohydrate 45g	**16%**
Dietary Fiber 9g	**32%**
Total Sugars 10g	
Includes 0g Added Sugars	**0%**
Protein 92g	**184%**
Vitamin D 0mcg	0%
Calcium 346mg	25%
Iron 12mg	70%
Potassium 2007mg	45%

*The % Daily Value (DV) tells you how much a nutrient in a serving of food contributes to a daily diet. 2,000 calories a day is used for general nutrition advice.

DIRECTIONS

Brown the ground beef over medium-high heat and chop into small pieces. When browned, add the water, parsley, chili powder, and garlic powder. Simmer uncovered over medium heat just until the liquid is gone (~8 minutes). Assemble by placing the crushed tortilla chips on a plate, followed by 1 cup of the meat mixture, then your desired amount of the cheese, onion, tomatoes, lettuce, and sour cream, along with your choice of salsa.

One-Pot Pasta

Prep Time: 15 Cook Time: 15 Recipe quantity:

INGREDIENTS

- 1 tbsp olive oil
- 1 medium yellow onion (8oz), diced
- 1 tsp garlic powder
- 1 (15oz) can no-salt-added diced tomatoes, puréed
- 1 (8oz) can no-salt-added tomato sauce
- 2 cups sodium-free chicken broth
- 1 tbsp dried basil
- 12 oz pasta (I prefer rotini)

Nutrition Facts

Nutrition Facts	
Serving size	
Amount Per Serving	
Calories	**1550**
	% Daily Value*
Total Fat 20g	**26%**
Saturated Fat 2g	**10%**
Trans Fat 0g	
Cholesterol 0mg	**0%**
Sodium 95mg	**4%**
Total Carbohydrate 291g	**106%**
Dietary Fiber 26g	**93%**
Total Sugars 29g	
Includes 2g Added Sugars	**4%**
Protein 54g	**108%**
Vitamin D 0mcg	0%
Calcium 107mg	8%
Iron 13mg	70%
Potassium 2752mg	60%

*The % Daily Value (DV) tells you how much a nutrient in a serving of food contributes to a daily diet. 2,000 calories a day is used for general nutrition advice.

DIRECTIONS

In a soup pot or Dutch oven, heat the olive oil and cook the onions until translucent (~5-7 minutes). Once cooked, add the remaining ingredients, ensuring that the pasta contacts the liquid. Bring to a boil, then simmer uncovered for approximately 10 minutes or until the pasta is cooked through and most of the liquid has been absorbed.

Parmesan Chicken

Prep Time: 10 Cook Time: 40 Recipe quantity:

INGREDIENTS

- **4 tbsp unsalted butter**
- **1 medium yellow onion (8oz), diced**
- **2 cups (10oz) skinless chicken breasts, cubed**
- **2 tsp Italian seasoning**
- **1 tsp black pepper**
- **1 tsp garlic powder**
- **½ cup (2oz) green onions, diced**
- **2½ cups sodium-free chicken broth**
- **1 cup uncooked long grain white rice**
- **½ cup heavy cream**
- **¼ cup Parmesan cheese**

Nutrition Facts

Nutrition Facts	
Serving size	
Amount Per Serving	
Calories	2090
	% Daily Value*
Total Fat 100g	**128%**
Saturated Fat 51g	**255%**
Trans Fat 0g	
Cholesterol 400mg	**133%**
Sodium 460mg	**20%**
Total Carbohydrate 177g	**64%**
Dietary Fiber 3g	**11%**
Total Sugars 19g	
Includes 2g Added Sugars	**4%**
Protein 96g	**192%**
Vitamin D 0mcg	0%
Calcium 388mg	30%
Iron 9mg	50%
Potassium 2100mg	45%

*The % Daily Value (DV) tells you how much a nutrient in a serving of food contributes to a daily diet. 2,000 calories a day is used for general nutrition advice.

DIRECTIONS

In a large skillet, melt the butter over medium-high heat. Add the onion and cook until translucent (~5-7 minutes). Add the chicken breast, Italian seasoning, and pepper. Stir often for 5 minutes, then add the garlic powder and cook for one additional minute. Add the green onions, chicken broth, and rice and stir to incorporate. Bring to a boil, then cover and simmer for approximately 20 minutes or until the rice has absorbed most of the liquid. Stir in the heavy cream and parmesan, continue to cook for 1 minute, then remove from the heat and allow to sit for five minutes prior to serving.

Parmesan Chicken Pasta

Prep Time: 10 Cook Time: 20 Recipe quantity:

INGREDIENTS

- 2 tbsp olive oil
- 1lb skinless chicken breast, sliced into ½" by 2" strips
- 1 medium yellow onion (8oz), diced
- 1 bell pepper (6oz), chopped
- 4 tbsp unsalted butter
- ½ tsp garlic powder
- 1 (14.5oz) can no-salt-added diced tomatoes, puréed
- 2 cups sodium-free chicken broth
- ½ tsp black pepper
- 1 tsp dried oregano
- ½ tsp cumin
- 1 tsp dried parsley
- 16oz penne, bowtie, or rotini pasta
- ½ cup Parmesan cheese

Nutrition Facts

Serving size

Amount Per Serving	
Calories	**3350**
	% Daily Value*
Total Fat 107g	**137%**
Saturated Fat 32g	**160%**
Trans Fat 0g	
Cholesterol 340mg	**113%**
Sodium 780mg	**34%**
Total Carbohydrate 372g	**135%**
Dietary Fiber 31g	**111%**
Total Sugars 30g	
Includes 0g Added Sugars	**0%**
Protein 186g	**372%**
Vitamin D 0mcg	0%
Calcium 560mg	45%
Iron 22mg	120%
Potassium 4006mg	90%

*The % Daily Value (DV) tells you how much a nutrient in a serving of food contributes to a daily diet. 2,000 calories a day is used for general nutrition advice.

DIRECTIONS

In a large skillet over medium-high heat, heat the olive oil then add the chicken, onion, and bell pepper and cook until the chicken has cooked through (~8-10 minutes). Add the butter, garlic powder, diced tomatoes, chicken broth, black pepper, oregano, cumin, and parsley to the skillet and heat to boiling. Add the uncooked pasta, then reduce the heat and simmer covered for 10-12 minutes or until the pasta has cooked through and most of the liquid has been absorbed. Turn off the heat and stir in the Parmesan cheese.

Parmesan Pasta

Prep Time: 10 Cook Time: 20 Recipe quantity:

INGREDIENTS

- 2 cups sodium-free chicken broth
- 2 tbsp unsalted butter
- ½ tsp black pepper
- ½ tsp garlic powder
- 1 cup milk
- 12 oz spaghetti
- ¼ cup Parmesan cheese
- 1 tsp dried parsley

Nutrition Facts

Serving size	
Amount Per Serving	
Calories	**1780**
	% Daily Value*
Total Fat 48g	**62%**
Saturated Fat 21g	**105%**
Trans Fat 0g	
Cholesterol 105mg	**35%**
Sodium 700mg	**30%**
Total Carbohydrate 270g	**98%**
Dietary Fiber 18g	**64%**
Total Sugars 20g	
Includes 0g Added Sugars	**0%**
Protein 69g	**138%**
Vitamin D 2mcg	10%
Calcium 793mg	60%
Iron 15mg	80%
Potassium 1923mg	40%

*The % Daily Value (DV) tells you how much a nutrient in a serving of food contributes to a daily diet. 2,000 calories a day is used for general nutrition advice.

DIRECTIONS

In a large skillet over medium heat, add the chicken broth, butter, black pepper, and garlic powder. Bring to a boil then add the milk and spaghetti, return to a boil, then simmer covered for 15 minutes, stirring occasionally. Add the Parmesan and parsley and stir to incorporate. If the sauce is too thick, add small amounts of milk until the desired consistency is reached. Allow to rest five minutes prior to serving.

Parmesan Pasta with Peas

Prep Time: 5 Cook Time: 15 Recipe quantity:

INGREDIENTS

- **16oz rotini or bowtie pasta**
- **3 tbsp unsalted butter**
- **1 cup (4oz) frozen peas**
- **½ cup Parmesan cheese**
- **½ tsp black pepper**

Nutrition Facts

Serving size	
Amount Per Serving	
Calories	**2210**
	% Daily Value*
Total Fat 53g	**68%**
Saturated Fat 20g	**100%**
Trans Fat 0g	
Cholesterol 85mg	**28%**
Sodium 610mg	**27%**
Total Carbohydrate 355g	**129%**
Dietary Fiber 30g	**107%**
Total Sugars 14g	
Includes 0g Added Sugars	**0%**
Protein 80g	**160%**
Vitamin D 0mcg	0%
Calcium 518mg	40%
Iron 20mg	110%
Potassium 1139mg	25%

*The % Daily Value (DV) tells you how much a nutrient in a serving of food contributes to a daily diet. 2,000 calories a day is used for general nutrition advice.

DIRECTIONS

Cook the pasta according to package directions. Meanwhile, in a large skillet melt the butter, then add the frozen peas and cook until heated thoroughly. When the pasta is finished cooking, drain and add the pasta along with the Parmesan cheese and black pepper. Stir thoroughly to incorporate, then serve.

Pasta Primavera

Prep Time: 15 Cook Time: 20 Recipe quantity:

INGREDIENTS

- **16 oz pasta (I prefer bowtie, rotini, or penne)**
- **2 tbsp olive oil**
- **1 medium yellow onion (8oz), chopped**
- **1 ½ cups (˜5oz) mushrooms, sliced**
- **1 cup (˜5oz) zucchini, peeled and sliced**
- **¼ cup (1oz) carrot, grated**
- **2 cups (10oz) cherry or grape tomatoes, halved**
- **¾ tsp garlic powder**
- **1 tbsp Italian seasoning**
- **½ tsp black pepper**
- **¾ cup Parmesan cheese**

Nutrition Facts

Serving size	
Amount Per Serving	
Calories	**2370**
	% Daily Value*
Total Fat 54g	**69%**
Saturated Fat 16g	**80%**
Trans Fat 0g	
Cholesterol 60mg	**20%**
Sodium 1080mg	**47%**
Total Carbohydrate 377g	**137%**
Dietary Fiber 39g	**139%**
Total Sugars 23g	
Includes 0g Added Sugars	**0%**
Protein 93g	**186%**
Vitamin D 0mcg	0%
Calcium 841mg	60%
Iron 24mg	130%
Potassium 3008mg	60%

*The % Daily Value (DV) tells you how much a nutrient in a serving of food contributes to a daily diet. 2,000 calories a day is used for general nutrition advice.

DIRECTIONS

Cook the pasta according to package directions. In a large skillet, heat the olive oil then cook the onion, mushrooms, zucchini, and carrot until the onion turns translucent (~5-7 minutes), stirring often. Add the tomatoes, garlic powder, Italian seasoning, and black pepper, and cook for 2 minutes, stirring often. Add the cooked pasta and mix well. Remove from the heat and stir in the Parmesan cheese.

Patty Melt

Prep Time: 15 Cook Time: 15 Recipe quantity:

INGREDIENTS

- ½ lb ground beef (I prefer 80:20 ground chuck)
- 1 tbsp sodium-free ketchup
- ½ tsp garlic powder
- ½ tsp black pepper
- 2 tbsp canola oil
- ½ medium yellow onion (4oz), sliced thinly
- 4 slices sandwich bread
- 2 slices Swiss cheese
- ¼ cup mayonnaise

Nutrition Facts

Serving size

Amount Per Serving	
Calories	**1660**
	% Daily Value*
Total Fat 128g	**164%**
Saturated Fat 32g	**160%**
Trans Fat 0g	
Cholesterol 240mg	**80%**
Sodium 960mg	**42%**
Total Carbohydrate 57g	**21%**
Dietary Fiber 9g	**32%**
Total Sugars 11g	
Includes 4g Added Sugars	**8%**
Protein 67g	**134%**
Vitamin D 0mcg	0%
Calcium 528mg	40%
Iron 11mg	60%
Potassium 767mg	15%

*The % Daily Value (DV) tells you how much a nutrient in a serving of food contributes to a daily diet. 2,000 calories a day is used for general nutrition advice.

DIRECTIONS

In a bowl, mix the ground beef with the ketchup, garlic powder, and black pepper. Shape the meat mixture into two ½"-thick patties. In a skillet, cook the onions in the oil until translucent (~5-7 minutes), then move the onions to a plate. Place the patties in a skillet and cook thoroughly (~4 minutes each side). Move the patties to the plate with the onions, then wipe the skillet clean and warm the skillet over medium heat. Assemble a patty melt by placing the cooked patty, onions, and 1 piece of Swiss cheese between two pieces of sandwich bread. Spread 1 tbsp of mayonnaise on the outside of one piece of bread, then lay that side of the patty melt down on the warmed skillet and place a small saucepan filled with water on top to compress the patty melt. After ~3 minutes, remove the saucepan and spread 1 tbsp of mayonnaise on the top of the melt, then flip and cook the other side of the patty melt for ~3 minutes. Repeat for the second patty melt. To serve, slice diagonally and enjoy.

Pizza (supreme)

Prep Time: 120 Cook Time: 25 Recipe quantity:

INGREDIENTS

Dough

- **3½ cups all-purpose flour**
- **2 tbsp olive oil**
- **1 tbsp granulated sugar**
- **1 packet instant yeast**
- **1 ½ cups lukewarm water**

Sauce

- **1 (8oz) can no-salt-added tomato sauce**
- **1 tbsp no-salt-added tomato paste**
- **1 tbsp dried oregano**
- **1 tsp garlic powder**
- **1 tsp paprika**

Toppings

- **½lb ground beef (I prefer 80:20 ground chuck)**
- **1 tsp olive oil**
- **1 cup mozzarella cheese**
- **½ medium yellow onion (4oz), sliced thinly**
- **½ cup (3oz) green bell pepper, sliced thinly**
- **½ cup (~1.5oz) mushrooms, sliced thinly**

Nutrition Facts

Serving size	
Amount Per Serving	
Calories	**2770**
	% Daily Value*
Total Fat 101g	**129%**
Saturated Fat 35g	**175%**
Trans Fat 0g	
Cholesterol 240mg	**80%**
Sodium 990mg	**43%**
Total Carbohydrate 356g	**129%**
Dietary Fiber 50g	**179%**
Total Sugars 27g	
Includes 0g Added Sugars	**0%**
Protein 117g	**234%**
Vitamin D 0mcg	0%
Calcium 885mg	70%
Iron 21mg	120%
Potassium 3425mg	70%

*The % Daily Value (DV) tells you how much a nutrient in a serving of food contributes to a daily diet. 2,000 calories a day is used for general nutrition advice.

DIRECTIONS

<u>Dough</u>: In a small bowl, mix the yeast, warm water, and sugar together, then allow to rest for 5 minutes. Pour into the bowl of a stand mixer. Add the olive oil and flour, then mix for approximately 2 minutes. Remove from the mixer and knead on a floured surface for 2-3 minutes. Allow the dough to rise for 1-2 hours at room temperature. Use a fist-sized piece of dough for an average (medium) sized thin-crust pizza (freeze any extra dough or use for a 2nd pizza). <u>Sauce</u>: mix all ingredients together. <u>Toppings</u>: brown the ground beef. Preheat the oven to 425°F. Roll out the dough, place it on a pan, and brush with olive oil. Layer on some sauce (freeze any excess sauce), followed by a layer of meat, then sprinkle ¾ cup of mozzarella over the meat. Add the onion, bell pepper, and mushrooms, followed by the remaining ¼ cup of mozzarella. Bake for 20 minutes or until the dough reaches the desired doneness.

Poppy Seed Chicken Pasta Salad

Prep Time: 30 Cook Time: 5 Recipe quantity:

INGREDIENTS

- **16 oz cooked and cooled rotini pasta**
- **2 cups (10oz) cooked and cooled skinless chicken breasts, shredded**
- **1½ cups (9oz) red grapes, halved**
- **1 cup (4oz) celery, diced**
- **½ cup (2oz) walnuts, chopped**
- **½ cup (2oz) green onions, diced**

Dressing

- **½ cup plain Greek yogurt**
- **½ cup mayonnaise**
- **3 tbsp apple cider vinegar**
- **3 tbsp honey**
- **2 tbsp granulated sugar**
- **1 tbsp poppy seeds**
- **1 tsp black pepper**

Nutrition Facts

Serving size

Amount Per Serving	
Calories	**3830**
	% Daily Value*
Total Fat 146g	**187%**
Saturated Fat 18g	**90%**
Trans Fat 0g	
Cholesterol 245mg	**82%**
Sodium 870mg	**38%**
Total Carbohydrate 476g	**173%**
Dietary Fiber 36g	**129%**
Total Sugars 130g	
Includes 0g Added Sugars	**0%**
Protein 148g	**296%**
Vitamin D 0mcg	0%
Calcium 566mg	45%
Iron 26mg	140%
Potassium 3049mg	60%

*The % Daily Value (DV) tells you how much a nutrient in a serving of food contributes to a daily diet. 2,000 calories a day is used for general nutrition advice.

DIRECTIONS

In a small bowl, mix together the Greek yogurt, mayonnaise, cider vinegar, honey, sugar, poppy seeds and black pepper. In a large bowl, mix together the pasta, chicken, grapes, celery, walnuts, and green onions. Pour the dressing mix over the top and toss to evenly coat. Place into the refrigerator for 1 hour to chill before serving.

Pork Chops

Prep Time: 10   Cook Time: 40   Recipe quantity:

INGREDIENTS

- 6 pork chops
- 4 tbsp unsalted butter
- 3 cups unseasoned breadcrumbs
- ¼ cup Parmesan cheese
- 1 tbsp dried oregano
- 1 ½ tsp dried sage
- 1 tsp dried rosemary
- 1 tsp black pepper

Nutrition Facts

Serving size	
Amount Per Serving	
Calories	**3040**
	% Daily Value*
Total Fat 92g	**118%**
Saturated Fat 32g	**160%**
Trans Fat 0g	
Cholesterol 1040mg	**347%**
Sodium 1470mg	**64%**
Total Carbohydrate 248g	**90%**
Dietary Fiber 13g	**46%**
Total Sugars 24g	
Includes 0g Added Sugars	**0%**
Protein 284g	**568%**
Vitamin D 9mcg	45%
Calcium 275mg	20%
Iron 22mg	120%
Potassium 4205mg	90%

*The % Daily Value (DV) tells you how much a nutrient in a serving of food contributes to a daily diet. 2,000 calories a day is used for general nutrition advice.

DIRECTIONS

Preheat the oven to 350°F. Melt the butter in a shallow dish just larger than one pork chop. Combine the breadcrumbs, Parmesan cheese, oregano, sage, rosemary, and black pepper in a medium-sized bowl and mix to combine. One at a time, dip the pork chop into the melted butter, drain, then transfer to the breadcrumbs mix and coat each pork chop thoroughly with crumbs. Place each coated pork chop onto a cookie sheet (preferably onto a footed wire cooling rack to allow for even cooking), then bake for 40 minutes or until the internal temperature of the pork chops reach at least 145°F.

Pork Ribs

Prep Time: 10 Cook Time: 240 Recipe quantity:

INGREDIENTS

- **2 slabs, unseasoned pork ribs**
- **1 cup brown sugar**
- **1 tbsp sodium-free chili powder**
- **1 tbsp cumin**
- **1 tsp black pepper**
- **1 tsp onion powder**
- **1 tsp garlic powder**
- **1 tsp paprika**
- **1 tsp dry ground mustard**

Nutrition Facts

Serving size	
Amount Per Serving	
Calories	**1860**
	% Daily Value*
Total Fat 52g	**67%**
Saturated Fat 15g	**75%**
Trans Fat 0g	
Cholesterol 350mg	**117%**
Sodium 260mg	**11%**
Total Carbohydrate 202g	**73%**
Dietary Fiber 1g	**4%**
Total Sugars 194g	
Includes 0g Added Sugars	**0%**
Protein 121g	**242%**
Vitamin D 0mcg	0%
Calcium 387mg	30%
Iron 10mg	60%
Potassium 221mg	4%

*The % Daily Value (DV) tells you how much a nutrient in a serving of food contributes to a daily diet. 2,000 calories a day is used for general nutrition advice.

DIRECTIONS

Unpackage the ribs and rinse under cold tap water. Mix all seasonings together in a small bowl. Sprinkle an ample amount of seasoning to each side of both slabs, rubbing it in with your hands. Collect any seasoning that falls off and re-apply. Place the ribs in the refrigerator for 1 hour. Preheat the grill to 250°F, and lay both slabs on the top rack, bone-side down. Grill for 4 hours (do not flip the slabs).

Potato Skins

Prep Time: 45 Cook Time: 20 Recipe quantity:

INGREDIENTS

- 3 large Russet potatoes
- 1lb ground beef (I prefer 80:20 ground chuck)
- ½ medium yellow onion (4oz), diced
- 1 tbsp Worcestershire sauce
- ½ tsp garlic powder
- ½ tsp sodium-free chili powder
- 1 tsp olive oil
- ¾ cup shredded cheddar cheese
- ¼ cup (1oz) green onions, sliced
- ½ cup sour cream

Nutrition Facts

Serving size

Amount Per Serving	
Calories	**2310**
	% Daily Value*
Total Fat 151g	**194%**
Saturated Fat 70g	**350%**
Trans Fat 0g	
Cholesterol 490mg	**163%**
Sodium 1060mg	**46%**
Total Carbohydrate 127g	**46%**
Dietary Fiber 9g	**32%**
Total Sugars 13g	
Includes 0g Added Sugars	**0%**
Protein 114g	**228%**
Vitamin D 0mcg	0%
Calcium 859mg	70%
Iron 14mg	80%
Potassium 3982mg	80%

*The % Daily Value (DV) tells you how much a nutrient in a serving of food contributes to a daily diet. 2,000 calories a day is used for general nutrition advice.

DIRECTIONS

Bake the potatoes until cooked throughout, then allow to cool to room temperature. When cool, slice each in half and scrape out most of the interior, leaving ½" of potato along with the skin. Preheat the oven to 350°F. In a large skillet, brown the ground beef with the onion over medium-high heat, then drain. Add the Worcestershire sauce, garlic powder, and chili powder to the meat, stir to combine, then turn off the heat. Brush some of the olive oil onto the inside of each potato skin, then spoon the meat mixture into the potato halves and then place each half on a foil-lined cookie sheet. Once all halves are filled, top each with the shredded cheddar. Bake at 350°F for 20 minutes or until the potato skins are heated through. Top with sour cream and green onions, then serve.

Potato Soup

Prep Time: 10 Cook Time: 20 Recipe quantity:

INGREDIENTS

- 4 slices low-sodium bacon, diced
- 1 medium yellow onion (8oz), chopped
- 1 tsp garlic powder
- ¼ cup all-purpose flour
- 2 cups sodium-free chicken broth
- 1½ cups milk
- 8 medium red potatoes, chopped into 1/2" cubes
- ½ cup heavy whipping cream
- 1 cup shredded cheddar cheese
- 2 tbsp minced chives
- 1 tsp black pepper
- ½ cup sour cream

Nutrition Facts

Serving size	
Amount Per Serving	
Calories	**1940**
	% Daily Value*
Total Fat 117g	**150%**
Saturated Fat 78g	**390%**
Trans Fat 0g	
Cholesterol 435mg	**145%**
Sodium 1250mg	**54%**
Total Carbohydrate 157g	**57%**
Dietary Fiber 10g	**36%**
Total Sugars 39g	
Includes 2g Added Sugars	**4%**
Protein 73g	**146%**
Vitamin D 3mcg	15%
Calcium 1545mg	120%
Iron 9mg	50%
Potassium 3902mg	80%

*The % Daily Value (DV) tells you how much a nutrient in a serving of food contributes to a daily diet. 2,000 calories a day is used for general nutrition advice.

DIRECTIONS

In a soup pan or Dutch oven, cook the bacon over medium-high heat until just prior to being crisp. Move the bacon to a paper towel and drain all but 1 tbsp of fat from the pan. Add the onion and cook over medium heat until it begins to turn translucent (~5-7 minutes). Add the garlic powder and flour and stir constantly until the flour begins to turn light brown. Add the chicken broth and milk, whisking to remove any clumps. Add the chopped potatoes, bring to a boil then quickly reduce the heat to simmer and cover. Cook until the potatoes collapse easily under minimal pressure, approximately 20 minutes. Using a spoon utensil, press the potatoes against the side of the pot to slightly mash them. Once completed, stir in the heavy cream, cheddar cheese, chives, and black pepper. Once the cheese has melted, turn off the heat and stir in the sour cream. Serve immediately.

Slow Cooker Pulled Pork

Prep Time: 10 Cook Time: 8 hrs Recipe quantity:

INGREDIENTS

- **4lbs pork shoulder (bone-in or boneless)**
- **1 cup sodium-free beef broth**
- **1 tsp ground black pepper**
- **1 tsp cumin**
- **1 tsp sodium-free chili powder**
- **1 tsp garlic powder**
- **1 tsp oregano**

Nutrition Facts

Serving size

Amount Per Serving	
Calories	**4220**
	% Daily Value*
Total Fat 320g	**410%**
Saturated Fat 112g	**560%**
Trans Fat 0g	
Cholesterol 1280mg	**427%**
Sodium 1200mg	**52%**
Total Carbohydrate 6g	**2%**
Dietary Fiber 0g	**0%**
Total Sugars 1g	
Includes 1g Added Sugars	**2%**
Protein 306g	**612%**
Vitamin D 0mcg	0%
Calcium 48mg	4%
Iron 87mg	480%
Potassium 441mg	10%

*The % Daily Value (DV) tells you how much a nutrient in a serving of food contributes to a daily diet. 2,000 calories a day is used for general nutrition advice.

DIRECTIONS

In a slow cooker, add the beef broth and all spices. Stir to combine. Add the pork shoulder and cook on the low setting for 8 hours. When finished cooking, remove any bones and shred the meat with utensils or your fingers. Once finished, return the meat to the cooker and stir to incorporate the juices before serving.

Quesadillas (Beef)

Prep Time: 15 Cook Time: 20 Recipe quantity:

INGREDIENTS

- ½lb ground beef (I prefer 80:20 ground chuck)
- ½ medium yellow onion (4oz), minced
- ½ bell pepper (~3oz), minced
- 1 tbsp sodium-free chili powder
- ½ tsp garlic powder
- 1 tsp dried parsley
- 1 tsp olive oil
- 10 corn tortillas
- 1 cup cheddar cheese

Nutrition Facts

Serving size	
Amount Per Serving	
Calories	**1680**
	% Daily Value*
Total Fat 95g	**122%**
Saturated Fat 43g	**215%**
Trans Fat 0g	
Cholesterol 280mg	**93%**
Sodium 950mg	**41%**
Total Carbohydrate 135g	**49%**
Dietary Fiber 18g	**64%**
Total Sugars 9g	
Includes 0g Added Sugars	**0%**
Protein 84g	**168%**
Vitamin D 0mcg	0%
Calcium 958mg	70%
Iron 6mg	35%
Potassium 1490mg	30%

*The % Daily Value (DV) tells you how much a nutrient in a serving of food contributes to a daily diet. 2,000 calories a day is used for general nutrition advice.

DIRECTIONS

In a skillet, brown the ground beef along with the minced onion and bell pepper over medium-high heat. While browning, mix the chili powder, garlic powder, and parsley in a medium bowl. Once browned, drain the meat then add it to the bowl of spices and stir to mix. Clear the skillet of any remaining juices, then heat the 1 tsp of olive oil over medium heat. Build the quesadilla by laying 1 tortilla in the pan, followed by a spoonful of meat mixture spread evenly over the tortilla, then 1 tbsp of cheddar cheese sprinkled over the meat, then top with a second corn tortilla. Place an empty saucepan filled half-full of water on top of the quesadilla while cooking to help keep the quesadilla flat. Flip the quesadilla after 2-3 minutes per side, placing the saucepan on top again. Repeat for the remaining quesadillas. Serve with a 2:1 mix of your favorite salsa and sour cream.

Slow Cooker Roast

Prep Time: 15 Cook Time: 8hrs Recipe quantity:

INGREDIENTS

- 4lbs chuck roast
- 2 cups beef broth
- 2 tbsp Worcestershire sauce
- 1 tsp onion powder
- 1 tsp garlic powder
- 1 tsp cumin
- 1 tsp black pepper
- 2 large Russet potatoes, roughly chopped
- 1 cup (~4.5oz) carrots, chopped
- 2 medium yellow onions (16oz), chopped
- 2 tsp cornstarch

Nutrition Facts

Serving size	
Amount Per Serving	
Calories	**2210**
	% Daily Value*
Total Fat 113g	**145%**
Saturated Fat 48g	**240%**
Trans Fat 0g	
Cholesterol 1120mg	**373%**
Sodium 1660mg	**72%**
Total Carbohydrate 130g	**47%**
Dietary Fiber 14g	**50%**
Total Sugars 30g	
Includes 2g Added Sugars	**4%**
Protein 568g	**1136%**
Vitamin D 0mcg	0%
Calcium 626mg	50%
Iron 40mg	220%
Potassium 3573mg	80%

*The % Daily Value (DV) tells you how much a nutrient in a serving of food contributes to a daily diet. 2,000 calories a day is used for general nutrition advice.

DIRECTIONS

In a slow cooker, add the beef broth, Worcestershire sauce, onion powder, garlic powder, cumin, and black pepper, then stir to combine. Add the roast, potatoes, carrots, and onions. Cook on low for 8 hours. When ready to serve, remove the roast, potatoes, carrots, and onions. Place ¼ cup of the juices in a small bowl and stir in the cornstarch. Pour the cornstarch mix into the slow cooker and slowly stir until the juices thicken to a gravy (~2-3 minutes). Add more cornstarch for a thicker gravy.

Roasted Chicken and Vegetables

Prep Time: 20 Cook Time: 60 Recipe quantity:

INGREDIENTS

- 3lbs chicken thighs, skinless
- 5 red potatoes, cut into 1" cubes
- 1 medium yellow onion (8oz), sliced
- 2 cups (10oz) cherry or grape tomatoes, halved
- 1 large red bell pepper (6oz), chopped
- 4 tbsp olive oil
- 1 tbsp balsamic vinegar
- 1 tsp garlic powder
- 1 tsp paprika
- ½ tsp black pepper
- 1 tsp dried basil
- 1 tsp cumin

Nutrition Facts	
Serving size	
Amount Per Serving	
Calories	**1760**
	% Daily Value*
Total Fat 77g	**99%**
Saturated Fat 14g	**70%**
Trans Fat 0g	
Cholesterol 320mg	**107%**
Sodium 200mg	**9%**
Total Carbohydrate 75g	**27%**
Dietary Fiber 15g	**54%**
Total Sugars 21g	
Includes 0g Added Sugars	**0%**
Protein 151g	**302%**
Vitamin D 0mcg	0%
Calcium 115mg	8%
Iron 9mg	50%
Potassium 3496mg	70%

*The % Daily Value (DV) tells you how much a nutrient in a serving of food contributes to a daily diet. 2,000 calories a day is used for general nutrition advice.

DIRECTIONS

Preheat the oven to 350°F. Set out two medium bowls. In one, add the vegetables and in the other, add the chicken. Drizzle the oil then the vinegar over both the vegetables and chicken, the toss each in the bowl to coat. After mixing, combine the spices in a small bowl and sprinkle the mix over the chicken and vegetables, then toss each again. Place a piece of aluminum foil over the bottom of a cookie sheet, then spray lightly with cooking spray. Arrange the chicken on the sheet, leaving 1-2" between each thigh. Lay the vegetables in the spaces between the chicken. Bake for 1 hour or until the chicken's internal temperature reaches 165°F. Allow to rest 10 minutes prior to serving.

Salisbury Steak

Prep Time: 15 Cook Time: 25 Recipe quantity:

INGREDIENTS

- 1lb ground beef (I prefer 80:20 ground chuck)
- 1 egg
- 1 tbsp no-salt-added tomato paste
- 1 tbsp yellow mustard
- 2 tbsp Worcestershire sauce
- ½ tsp garlic powder
- ¼ cup unseasoned breadcrumbs
- ½ tsp black pepper
- ¾ cup water

Gravy

- 2 tbsp unsalted butter
- 1 medium yellow onion (8oz), diced
- 1 cup (3oz) mushrooms, sliced
- 3 tbsp all-purpose flour
- ½ tsp dried thyme
- 1 tbsp low-sodium soy sauce
- 1 ½ cups sodium-free beef broth

Nutrition Facts

Serving size	
Amount Per Serving	
Calories	**1750**
	% Daily Value*
Total Fat 115g	**147%**
Saturated Fat 46g	**230%**
Trans Fat 0g	
Cholesterol 535mg	**178%**
Sodium 1110mg	**48%**
Total Carbohydrate 71g	**26%**
Dietary Fiber 6g	**21%**
Total Sugars 28g	
Includes 2g Added Sugars	**4%**
Protein 96g	**192%**
Vitamin D 1mcg	4%
Calcium 119mg	10%
Iron 16mg	90%
Potassium 2631mg	60%

*The % Daily Value (DV) tells you how much a nutrient in a serving of food contributes to a daily diet. 2,000 calories a day is used for general nutrition advice.

DIRECTIONS

In a bowl, combine all non-gravy ingredients together and mix well (the mixture will be slightly soggy). Form approximately 4-5 round balls and shape them into patties. Cook the patties over medium heat in a skillet for 5 minutes per side and then remove them from the skillet. To make the gravy, in a wide skillet melt the butter over medium-high heat. Add the onions and mushrooms and stir often until the onions turn translucent (~5-7 minutes). Add the flour and continue to stir. Once the flour begins to brown, add the thyme and cook another 30 seconds. Stir in the soy sauce and beef broth and bring to a boil, then reduce the heat to a simmer. Add the patties back to the gravy and cook covered over medium heat for an additional 10 minutes.

Sheet Pan Nachos

Prep Time: 20 Cook Time: 5 Recipe quantity:

INGREDIENTS

- 1lb ground beef (I prefer 80:20 ground chuck)
- ½ cup water
- 1 tbsp sodium-free chili powder
- 1 tbsp dried parsley
- ½ tsp garlic powder
- 1 large (14oz) bag, unsalted tortilla chips
- 1 medium yellow onion (8oz), diced
- ½ cup (~3.5oz) roma tomatoes, diced
- ½ cup (~1.5oz) jalapeno peppers, diced
- 1 (15oz) can no-salt-added black beans, drained and rinsed
- 1 tbsp dried cilantro
- 1 cup sour cream
- 1 cup shredded cheddar cheese

Nutrition Facts	
Serving size	
Amount Per Serving	
Calories	3470
	% Daily Value*
Total Fat 212g	272%
Saturated Fat 94g	470%
Trans Fat 0g	
Cholesterol 600mg	200%
Sodium 1200mg	52%
Total Carbohydrate 208g	76%
Dietary Fiber 30g	107%
Total Sugars 21g	
Includes 0g Added Sugars	0%
Protein 153g	306%
Vitamin D 0mcg	0%
Calcium 1356mg	100%
Iron 23mg	130%
Potassium 4519mg	100%

*The % Daily Value (DV) tells you how much a nutrient in a serving of food contributes to a daily diet. 2,000 calories a day is used for general nutrition advice.

DIRECTIONS

In a medium skillet, brown the ground beef over medium-high heat. Once browned, add the water, chili powder, parsley, and garlic powder. Simmer just until the liquid is gone, then remove from the heat. On an ungreased sheet pan, spread out the tortilla chips (more chips mean more nachos, but too many chips may leave many of the chips without any topping). Sprinkle the meat mixture over the chips. Then sprinkle the onion, roma tomatoes, jalapenos, black beans, and cilantro. Sprinkle the cheddar cheese over the top of all ingredients, then place under the broiler for 2-3 minutes or until the cheese has melted. While broiling, place the sour cream into a sandwich bag, seal the bag, then cut the very tip of one corner from the bag so that a small ⅛" hole is formed. When finished broiling, squeeze the sour cream over the chips. Serve immediately.

Sloppy Joes

Prep Time: 5 Cook Time: 30 Recipe quantity:

INGREDIENTS

- **1lb ground beef (I prefer 80:20 ground chuck)**
- **1 cup sodium-free ketchup**
- **¼ cup water**
- **2 tbsp brown sugar**
- **2 tsp Worcestershire sauce**
- **2 tsp yellow mustard**
- **½ tsp garlic powder**
- **½ tsp onion powder**
- **½ tsp black pepper**
- **½ tsp cumin**

Nutrition Facts

Serving size	
Amount Per Serving	
Calories	**1650**
	% Daily Value*
Total Fat 88g	**113%**
Saturated Fat 36g	**180%**
Trans Fat 0g	
Cholesterol 320mg	**107%**
Sodium 580mg	**25%**
Total Carbohydrate 109g	**40%**
Dietary Fiber 0g	**0%**
Total Sugars 106g	
Includes 32g Added Sugars	**64%**
Protein 77g	**154%**
Vitamin D 0mcg	0%
Calcium 71mg	6%
Iron 13mg	70%
Potassium 2852mg	60%

*The % Daily Value (DV) tells you how much a nutrient in a serving of food contributes to a daily diet. 2,000 calories a day is used for general nutrition advice.

DIRECTIONS

In a large skillet, brown the ground beef over medium-high heat and chop into small pieces. Once browned, add the remaining ingredients and stir to incorporate. Bring to a boil, then simmer for 20 minutes or until only a minimal amount of liquid remains. Serve with your favorite hamburger bun.

Smothered Baked Potatoes

Prep Time: 20 Cook Time: 60 Recipe quantity:

INGREDIENTS

- 3 large Russet potatoes
- ½lb ground beef (I prefer 80:20 ground chuck)
- 2 tbsp Worcestershire sauce
- 2 tbsp unsalted butter, melted
- 1 medium yellow onion (8oz), chopped
- 2 cups (~5oz) mushrooms, sliced
- 1 cup (6oz) bell pepper, chopped
- ½ cup (2oz) green onions, sliced
- 1 cup shredded cheddar cheese

Nutrition Facts	
Serving size	
Amount Per Serving	
Calories	1960
	% Daily Value*
Total Fat 105g	**135%**
Saturated Fat 50g	**250%**
Trans Fat 0g	
Cholesterol 310mg	**103%**
Sodium 1330mg	**58%**
Total Carbohydrate 177g	**64%**
Dietary Fiber 19g	**68%**
Total Sugars 24g	
Includes 0g Added Sugars	**0%**
Protein 92g	**184%**
Vitamin D 0mcg	0%
Calcium 984mg	80%
Iron 12mg	70%
Potassium 4995mg	110%

*The % Daily Value (DV) tells you how much a nutrient in a serving of food contributes to a daily diet. 2,000 calories a day is used for general nutrition advice.

DIRECTIONS

Bake the potatoes (in the oven or microwave) until soft throughout. When halfway done baking, brown the ground beef in a medium skillet over medium-high heat. When browned, mix in the Worcestershire sauce and then cook for 1 additional minute. Remove the ground beef and then drain and wipe the skillet. Melt the butter and then cook the onion, mushrooms, and pepper until cooked through, approximately 5-7 minutes. When the potatoes are done baking, slice them in half and arrange them in a greased 8"x8" (or larger if needed) baking dish. Spoon the meat mixture over the top and then sprinkle with the green onions and cheese. Broil for 2-3 minutes or until the cheese has melted.

Spaghetti with Meat Sauce

Prep Time: 10 Cook Time: 15 Recipe quantity:

INGREDIENTS

- 16 ounces spaghetti
- ¼lb ground beef (I prefer 80:20 ground chuck)
- ½ medium yellow onion (4oz), diced
- ¼ cup (~1.5oz) bell pepper, diced
- 1 tbsp Italian seasoning
- ½ tsp garlic powder
- ½ tsp black pepper
- 2 (14.5oz) cans no-salt-added diced tomatoes, puréed
- 2 (8oz) cans no-salt-added tomato sauce

Nutrition Facts

Serving size

Amount Per Serving	
Calories	**2220**
	% Daily Value*
Total Fat 30g	**38%**
Saturated Fat 9g	**45%**
Trans Fat 0g	
Cholesterol 80mg	**27%**
Sodium 270mg	**12%**
Total Carbohydrate 396g	**144%**
Dietary Fiber 40g	**143%**
Total Sugars 48g	
Includes 0g Added Sugars	**0%**
Protein 92g	**184%**
Vitamin D 0mcg	0%
Calcium 176mg	15%
Iron 23mg	130%
Potassium 3894mg	80%

*The % Daily Value (DV) tells you how much a nutrient in a serving of food contributes to a daily diet. 2,000 calories a day is used for general nutrition advice.

DIRECTIONS

Cook the spaghetti according to package directions, then drain. While the spaghetti is being prepared, brown the ground beef over medium-high heat along with the diced onion and green pepper in a saucepan. Once cooked, add the Italian seasoning, garlic powder, and black pepper. Stir to mix, then cook for 1 minute. Add the diced tomatoes and tomato sauce. Stir to mix, bring to a boil, then simmer uncovered while stirring occasionally. To serve, place a heaping mound of spaghetti on a plate and then spoon on the sauce. Top with Parmesan cheese, if desired.

Spinach and Bacon Frittata

Prep Time: 15 Cook Time: 40 Recipe quantity:

INGREDIENTS

- 6 slices low-sodium bacon, diced
- 3 cups (5oz) spinach leaves (stems removed)
- 8 eggs
- ¼ cup heavy whipping cream
- ½ tsp onion powder
- ¼ tsp garlic powder
- ½ tsp black pepper
- 2/3 cup shredded Swiss cheese

Nutrition Facts	
Serving size	
Amount Per Serving	
Calories	1280
	% Daily Value*
Total Fat 98g	126%
Saturated Fat 51g	255%
Trans Fat 0g	
Cholesterol 1665mg	555%
Sodium 1290mg	56%
Total Carbohydrate 14g	5%
Dietary Fiber 3g	11%
Total Sugars 4g	
Includes 0g Added Sugars	0%
Protein 91g	182%
Vitamin D 8mcg	40%
Calcium 1164mg	90%
Iron 14mg	80%
Potassium 1350mg	30%

*The % Daily Value (DV) tells you how much a nutrient in a serving of food contributes to a daily diet. 2,000 calories a day is used for general nutrition advice.

DIRECTIONS

Preheat the oven to 350°F. In a medium skillet, cook the bacon until just prior to crispy. Remove from the pan and drain all but 1 tsp bacon grease. Add the spinach leaves and cook for 2 minutes or until wilted thoroughly. In a large bowl, beat the eggs thoroughly then add the remaining ingredients to the bowl as well as the cooked bacon and spinach and stir to combine. Pour the mix into a greased 8x8" baking dish and stir to ensure ingredients are evenly distributed. Bake for 35 minutes or until the center of the frittata is cooked through. Allow to rest for 5 minutes prior to serving.

Steak Bites

Prep Time: 10 Cook Time: 15 Recipe quantity:

INGREDIENTS

- 1 tbsp olive oil
- 2lbs strip steak or sirloin, cut into 3/4" cubes
- 2 tbsp low-sodium soy sauce
- 1 tsp black pepper
- 2 tbsp unsalted butter
- 1 tsp garlic powder
- 1 tsp cumin
- 1 tbsp dried parsley

Nutrition Facts	
Serving size	
Amount Per Serving	
Calories	**1280**
	% Daily Value*
Total Fat 92g	**118%**
Saturated Fat 34g	**170%**
Trans Fat 0g	
Cholesterol 590mg	**197%**
Sodium 630mg	**27%**
Total Carbohydrate 36g	**13%**
Dietary Fiber 0g	**0%**
Total Sugars 26g	
Includes 0g Added Sugars	**0%**
Protein 283g	**566%**
Vitamin D 0mcg	0%
Calcium 260mg	20%
Iron 24mg	130%
Potassium 215mg	4%

*The % Daily Value (DV) tells you how much a nutrient in a serving of food contributes to a daily diet. 2,000 calories a day is used for general nutrition advice.

DIRECTIONS

In a wide skillet over medium-high heat, heat the olive oil and then add the steak. Cook for approximately 8-10 minutes to cook through, stirring often. Next, add the soy sauce and black pepper, then stir to coat the steak pieces. In a separate small bowl, melt the butter, then add the garlic powder and cumin and stir to combine. Add the butter to the skillet and stir to coat the steak pieces. Sprinkle with parsley and serve immediately.

Stroganoff

Prep Time: 10 Cook Time: 20 Recipe quantity:

INGREDIENTS

- **1lb ground beef (I prefer 80:20 ground chuck)**
- **1 medium yellow onion (8oz), diced**
- **1 tbsp olive oil**
- **1 cup (3oz) mushrooms, sliced**
- **½ tsp garlic powder**
- **1 cup sodium-free beef broth**
- **½ cup heavy cream**
- **½ cup sour cream**
- **12oz egg noodles**

Nutrition Facts

Serving size	
Amount Per Serving	
Calories	**3190**
	% Daily Value*
Total Fat 168g	**215%**
Saturated Fat 80g	**400%**
Trans Fat 0g	
Cholesterol 560mg	**187%**
Sodium 550mg	**24%**
Total Carbohydrate 268g	**97%**
Dietary Fiber 15g	**54%**
Total Sugars 17g	
Includes 0g Added Sugars	**0%**
Protein 135g	**270%**
Vitamin D 8mcg	40%
Calcium 389mg	30%
Iron 16mg	90%
Potassium 3091mg	70%

*The % Daily Value (DV) tells you how much a nutrient in a serving of food contributes to a daily diet. 2,000 calories a day is used for general nutrition advice.

DIRECTIONS

Brown the ground beef over medium-high heat along with the diced onion. Once browned, remove it from the pan and drain the liquid. In the same pan, add the olive oil, mushrooms, and garlic powder. Cook over medium-high heat for 5 minutes, stirring often. Return the browned ground beef to the pan and add the beef broth and heavy cream. Heat to boiling, then simmer uncovered for 5-7 minutes or until the sauce thickens. While simmering, cook the egg noodles according to package directions, then drain. Remove the meat mixture from the heat and stir in the sour cream. Serve over the cooked egg noodles.

Stroganoff #2

Prep Time: 10 Cook Time: 25 Recipe quantity:

INGREDIENTS

- 12 oz rotini pasta noodles
- 1lb ground beef (I prefer 80:20 ground chuck)
- ½ medium yellow onion (4oz), diced
- 1 tbsp olive oil
- 1 cup (3oz) mushrooms, sliced
- ½ tsp garlic powder
- 2 tbsp all-purpose flour
- 1 cup sodium-free beef broth
- 1 cup heavy cream
- 1 tbsp Worcestershire sauce
- ½ tsp black pepper
- ½ cup sour cream

Nutrition Facts

Serving size	
Amount Per Serving	
Calories	**3500**
	% Daily Value*
Total Fat 198g	**254%**
Saturated Fat 101g	**505%**
Trans Fat 0g	
Cholesterol 680mg	**227%**
Sodium 640mg	**28%**
Total Carbohydrate 296g	**108%**
Dietary Fiber 22g	**79%**
Total Sugars 30g	
Includes 1g Added Sugars	**2%**
Protein 128g	**256%**
Vitamin D 0mcg	0%
Calcium 358mg	30%
Iron 25mg	140%
Potassium 3170mg	70%

*The % Daily Value (DV) tells you how much a nutrient in a serving of food contributes to a daily diet. 2,000 calories a day is used for general nutrition advice.

DIRECTIONS

Prepare the noodles according to package directions, then drain. Meanwhile, in a wide skillet, brown the ground beef over medium-high heat along with the diced onion. Once browned, drain the liquid then heat the olive oil. Add the sliced mushrooms and garlic powder and continue to cook, stirring often, for another 5 minutes. Stir in the flour, then add the beef broth, heavy cream, Worcestershire sauce, and black pepper. Bring to a boil, then reduce the heat and simmer uncovered for 10 minutes. After simmering, turn off the heat and stir in the sour cream. Stir in the noodles and allow to rest 5 minutes prior to serving.

Stuffed Bell Peppers

Prep Time: 15 Cook Time: 30 Recipe quantity:

INGREDIENTS

- **1 cup instant rice**
- **4 bell peppers**
- **¾lb ground beef (I prefer 80:20 ground chuck)**
- **½ medium yellow onion (4oz), diced**
- **2 (8oz) cans no-salt-added tomato sauce**
- **½ tsp black pepper**
- **½ tsp cumin**
- **½ tsp garlic powder**
- **½ tsp onion powder**
- **¼ cup cheddar cheese**

Nutrition Facts	
Serving size	
Amount Per Serving	
Calories	**1560**
	% Daily Value*
Total Fat 75g	**96%**
Saturated Fat 33g	**165%**
Trans Fat 0g	
Cholesterol 270mg	**90%**
Sodium 500mg	**22%**
Total Carbohydrate 133g	**48%**
Dietary Fiber 17g	**61%**
Total Sugars 38g	
Includes 0g Added Sugars	**0%**
Protein 85g	**170%**
Vitamin D 0mcg	0%
Calcium 269mg	20%
Iron 15mg	80%
Potassium 2803mg	60%

*The % Daily Value (DV) tells you how much a nutrient in a serving of food contributes to a daily diet. 2,000 calories a day is used for general nutrition advice.

DIRECTIONS

Preheat the oven to 350°F. Cook the instant rice according to package directions. Remove the tops from the bell peppers and scrape out the seeds and linings. In a large skillet, brown the ground beef over medium-high heat along with the onion, then drain. To the meat and onion mix, add the cooked rice, tomato sauce, black pepper, cumin, garlic powder, and onion powder, and stir to mix. Heat until boiling, then turn off the heat and spoon the mix into the peppers. Stand the stuffed peppers upright in a muffin pan, then place the muffin pan in a 9"x13" baking dish. Bake for 30 minutes, sprinkling the ¼ cup cheddar cheese on each when 5 minutes are remaining in the bake time.

Swiss Steak

Prep Time: 15 Cook Time: 75 Recipe quantity:

INGREDIENTS

- 2 tbsp olive oil + 1 tbsp
- 2lbs top or bottom round steak, tenderized and sliced to 1/2" thick
- ½ cup all-purpose flour
- 1 tbsp black pepper
- 1 medium yellow onion (8oz), sliced into ¼" strips
- 1 tsp garlic powder
- 1 tbsp no-salt-added tomato paste
- 1 (14.5oz) can no-salt-added diced tomatoes, puréed
- 2 cups sodium-free beef broth
- 2 tsp Italian seasoning
- 1 tbsp Worcestershire sauce
- 1 tbsp dried parsley

Nutrition Facts

Serving size

Amount Per Serving	
Calories	**1600**
	% Daily Value*
Total Fat 98g	**126%**
Saturated Fat 30g	**150%**
Trans Fat 0g	
Cholesterol 560mg	**187%**
Sodium 770mg	**33%**
Total Carbohydrate 84g	**31%**
Dietary Fiber 11g	**39%**
Total Sugars 23g	
Includes 2g Added Sugars	**4%**
Protein 292g	**584%**
Vitamin D 0mcg	0%
Calcium 317mg	25%
Iron 36mg	200%
Potassium 2594mg	60%

*The % Daily Value (DV) tells you how much a nutrient in a serving of food contributes to a daily diet. 2,000 calories a day is used for general nutrition advice.

DIRECTIONS

In a wide skillet, heat 2 tbsp of the olive oil over medium heat. Place the flour on a plate or in a wide dish, then add the black pepper and stir to combine. Dredge both sides of the steak pieces in the flour mix, then add the steak to the hot skillet. Cook 3-4 minutes per side. Once all steak pieces have been cooked on both sides, move them to a plate. Heat the remaining tbsp of olive oil in the skillet and cook the onion slices - stirring often - until they turn translucent (~7-10 minutes). Add the garlic powder and tomato paste and cook for 1 minute, stirring often. Add the remaining ingredients and bring to a boil, then reduce to a simmer. Add the steaks back to the skillet and press down into the sauce. Cover and simmer over medium-low heat for 1 hour. Serve as prepared, or serve over rice or noodles.

Taco Chili Soup

Prep Time: 15 Cook Time: 70 Recipe quantity:

INGREDIENTS

- 1lb ground beef (I prefer 80:20 ground chuck)
- 1 medium yellow onion (8oz), diced
- 3 cups sodium-free beef broth
- 1 tsp garlic powder
- 1 tbsp sodium-free chili powder
- 1 tsp cumin
- ½ tsp dried oregano
- ½ tsp paprika
- 1 tsp onion powder
- ½ tsp black pepper
- 2 (14.5oz) cans no-salt-added diced tomatoes, puréed
- 1 (10oz) can no-salt-added diced tomatoes with green chilis
- 1 (15oz) can no-salt-added kidney beans, drained
- 1 (15oz) can no-salt-added black beans, drained
- 1 (15oz) can no-salt-added corn, drained

Nutrition Facts	
Serving size	
Amount Per Serving	
Calories	2350
	% Daily Value*
Total Fat 88g	**113%**
Saturated Fat 36g	**180%**
Trans Fat 0g	
Cholesterol 320mg	**107%**
Sodium 520mg	**23%**
Total Carbohydrate 212g	**77%**
Dietary Fiber 62g	**221%**
Total Sugars 42g	
Includes 3g Added Sugars	**6%**
Protein 144g	**288%**
Vitamin D 0mcg	0%
Calcium 543mg	40%
Iron 29mg	160%
Potassium 7839mg	170%

*The % Daily Value (DV) tells you how much a nutrient in a serving of food contributes to a daily diet. 2,000 calories a day is used for general nutrition advice.

DIRECTIONS

In a soup pot, brown the ground beef over medium-high heat along with the onion. Once browned, add all remaining ingredients. Bring to a boil, then reduce heat, cover, and simmer for one hour, stirring occasionally. To make it even better, sprinkle a little cheddar cheese on top of each bowl when serving.

Tangy Chicken Wings

Prep Time: 15 Cook Time: 40 Recipe quantity:

INGREDIENTS

- **4lbs skinless chicken wings, separated into wingettes and drumettes**
- **2 tbsp unsalted butter**
- **½ cup low-sodium soy sauce**
- **½ cup honey**
- **¼ cup rice wine vinegar**
- **1 tsp garlic powder**
- **1 tbsp dried ginger**

Nutrition Facts

Serving size	
Amount Per Serving	
Calories	**2100**
	% Daily Value*
Total Fat 42g	**54%**
Saturated Fat 14g	**70%**
Trans Fat 0g	
Cholesterol 350mg	**117%**
Sodium 600mg	**26%**
Total Carbohydrate 250g	**91%**
Dietary Fiber 0g	**0%**
Total Sugars 240g	
Includes 0g Added Sugars	**0%**
Protein 157g	**314%**
Vitamin D 0mcg	0%
Calcium 2mg	0%
Iron 8mg	45%
Potassium 1472mg	30%

*The % Daily Value (DV) tells you how much a nutrient in a serving of food contributes to a daily diet. 2,000 calories a day is used for general nutrition advice.

DIRECTIONS

Place the cut wing pieces on a wire rack and cook in the oven on 400°F until the internal temperature of the wings reaches 165°F (~30-35 minutes). While cooking, add the remaining ingredients to a medium saucepan, bring to boiling, then simmer for 10-15 minutes until the sauce thickens. When the wing pieces are done cooking, remove them from the oven. Dip each wing piece in the sauce and enjoy immediately.

Vegetable Beef Soup

Prep Time: 15 Cook Time: 45 Recipe quantity:

INGREDIENTS

- 1lb ground beef (I prefer 80:20 ground chuck)
- 4 cups sodium-free chicken broth
- 2 (14.5oz) cans, no-salt-added diced tomatoes, puréed
- 1 (8oz) can no-salt-added tomato sauce
- ½ medium yellow onion (4oz), diced
- ¼ cup (1oz) carrot, shredded, or grated
- 1 (15oz) can no-salt-added green beans, drained
- 1 cup (4oz) frozen peas
- 1 (15oz) can no-salt-added corn, drained
- 1 tsp garlic powder
- ½ tsp black pepper
- 1 tsp dried basil

Nutrition Facts	
Serving size	
Amount Per Serving	
Calories	1660
	% Daily Value*
Total Fat 88g	113%
Saturated Fat 36g	180%
Trans Fat 0g	
Cholesterol 320mg	107%
Sodium 560mg	24%
Total Carbohydrate 97g	35%
Dietary Fiber 24g	86%
Total Sugars 52g	
Includes 4g Added Sugars	8%
Protein 106g	212%
Vitamin D 0mcg	0%
Calcium 283mg	20%
Iron 17mg	90%
Potassium 5347mg	110%

*The % Daily Value (DV) tells you how much a nutrient in a serving of food contributes to a daily diet. 2,000 calories a day is used for general nutrition advice.

DIRECTIONS

In a small skillet, brown the ground beef over medium-high heat and chop into very small pieces. When done, drain the meat and set aside until the last 5 minutes of cooking. Add the chicken broth to a soup pot and bring to boil. Stir in the remaining ingredients. Bring back to a boil, then reduce the heat to medium-low and simmer uncovered for 30 minutes, after which add the cooked ground beef to the soup and cook for an additional 5 minutes before serving.

Breakfast

Belgian Waffles

Prep Time: 10 Cook Time: 15 Recipe quantity:

INGREDIENTS

- 2¼ cups all-purpose flour
- 1/2 cup sugar
- 1 tbsp sodium-free baking powder
- 1½ cups milk
- 1 cup unsalted butter, melted
- 3 eggs, beaten
- 1 tsp vanilla extract

Nutrition Facts	
Serving size	
Amount Per Serving	
Calories	3320
	% Daily Value*
Total Fat 203g	**260%**
Saturated Fat 78g	**390%**
Trans Fat 0g	
Cholesterol 850mg	**283%**
Sodium 370mg	**16%**
Total Carbohydrate 321g	**117%**
Dietary Fiber 27g	**96%**
Total Sugars 114g	
Includes 0g Added Sugars	**0%**
Protein 57g	**114%**
Vitamin D 6mcg	30%
Calcium 1500mg	120%
Iron 12mg	70%
Potassium 3480mg	70%

*The % Daily Value (DV) tells you how much a nutrient in a serving of food contributes to a daily diet. 2,000 calories a day is used for general nutrition advice.

DIRECTIONS

Turn on the waffle maker so that it is hot when ready to use. Coat the waffle maker with cooking spray if recommended. Combine dry ingredients (flour, sugar, baking powder) in a medium-sized bowl and stir to mix. Combine the wet ingredients (milk, melted butter, beaten eggs, and vanilla) in a separate bowl and stir to mix. Pour the wet ingredients into the dry ingredient bowl and stir gently to combine (do not stir too much). Pour approximately ½ cup (or as recommended by the waffle-maker manufacturer) of batter into the waffle maker and cook according to manufacturer directions. Enjoy with syrup, butter, chocolate chips, fruit, or your own favorite toppings.

French Toast

Prep Time: 10 Cook Time: 10 Recipe quantity:

INGREDIENTS

- **1 cup canola or vegetable oil for frying**
- **¼ cup milk**
- **2 eggs**
- **½ tsp vanilla extract**
- **3 slices sandwich bread**

Nutrition Facts

Serving size	
Amount Per Serving	
Calories	**600**
	% Daily Value*
Total Fat 42g	**54%**
Saturated Fat 7g	**35%**
Trans Fat 0g	
Cholesterol 380mg	**127%**
Sodium 500mg	**22%**
Total Carbohydrate 38g	**14%**
Dietary Fiber 6g	**21%**
Total Sugars 6g	
Includes 6g Added Sugars	**12%**
Protein 26g	**52%**
Vitamin D 3mcg	15%
Calcium 285mg	20%
Iron 4mg	20%
Potassium 240mg	6%

*The % Daily Value (DV) tells you how much a nutrient in a serving of food contributes to a daily diet. 2,000 calories a day is used for general nutrition advice.

DIRECTIONS

Heat the oil over medium-high heat. While heating, in a flat-bottomed container just larger than a piece of bread, beat the eggs with the milk and vanilla extract. Dip one piece of bread in the egg mixture to coat both sides. When the oil has reached approximately 350°F, carefully place the bread in the oil. Cook each side for approximately 2 minutes. Repeat for all bread slices. When finished, cut the bread diagonally and top with any combination of butter, syrup, whipped cream, powdered sugar, or your favorite fruit.

Omelet Bowl

Prep Time: 10 Cook Time: 15 Recipe quantity:

INGREDIENTS

- 1 tbsp olive oil
- 2 slices low-sodium bacon, diced
- ½ medium yellow onion (4oz), diced
- ½ green bell pepper (~3oz), diced
- 1 medium potato, cooked and diced
- 1 cup (3oz) mushrooms, sliced
- 4 eggs, well beaten
- ¼ cup shredded cheddar cheese
- ½ tsp black pepper

Nutrition Facts	
Serving size	
Amount Per Serving	
Calories	700
	% Daily Value*
Total Fat 47g	**60%**
Saturated Fat 18g	**90%**
Trans Fat 0g	
Cholesterol 780mg	**260%**
Sodium 660mg	**29%**
Total Carbohydrate 28g	**10%**
Dietary Fiber 5g	**18%**
Total Sugars 5g	
Includes 0g Added Sugars	**0%**
Protein 44g	**88%**
Vitamin D 4mcg	20%
Calcium 347mg	25%
Iron 7mg	40%
Potassium 1143mg	25%

*The % Daily Value (DV) tells you how much a nutrient in a serving of food contributes to a daily diet. 2,000 calories a day is used for general nutrition advice.

DIRECTIONS

Heat the oil in a medium-sized skillet over medium heat. Add the diced bacon along with the onion and bell pepper to the skillet, stirring often. About 5 minutes in, add the diced potato and mushrooms and continue to stir often. When the mushrooms have cooked through (~3-4 minutes), pour in the eggs. Add the cheese and black pepper and begin to scrape around the bottom of the pan with a spatula as the eggs start to firm up. Once no liquid remains in the egg, remove from the heat and serve.

Sides

Au Gratin Potatoes

Prep Time: 15 Cook Time: 80 Recipe quantity:

INGREDIENTS

- 2 tbsp unsalted butter
- ¼ cup all-purpose flour
- 1½ cups milk
- 2 cups cheddar cheese
- ¼ tsp garlic powder
- ½ tsp black pepper
- 4 large Russet potatoes or 10-12 red potatoes, halved and then cut to ⅛" thick slices
- 1 medium yellow onion (8oz), chopped
- ¼ cup Parmesan cheese

Nutrition Facts

Serving size	
Amount Per Serving	
Calories	**2020**
	% Daily Value*
Total Fat 114g	**146%**
Saturated Fat 68g	**340%**
Trans Fat 0g	
Cholesterol 345mg	**115%**
Sodium 1830mg	**80%**
Total Carbohydrate 175g	**64%**
Dietary Fiber 12g	**43%**
Total Sugars 26g	
Includes 0g Added Sugars	**0%**
Protein 93g	**186%**
Vitamin D 3mcg	15%
Calcium 2358mg	180%
Iron 8mg	45%
Potassium 3519mg	70%

*The % Daily Value (DV) tells you how much a nutrient in a serving of food contributes to a daily diet. 2,000 calories a day is used for general nutrition advice.

DIRECTIONS

In a saucepan, melt the butter over medium heat and then whisk in the flour. Slowly pour in the milk while whisking constantly, ensuring no lumps remain. Once the milk is simmering, add the cheddar cheese in batches and stir constantly until the cheese has melted. Turn off the heat, add in the garlic powder and black pepper, and stir to mix. Preheat the oven to 375°F. Toss the onion and potato slices in a medium bowl and then pour into a greased 9"x13" baking dish. Pour the cheese sauce over the potatoes and onions, mix to incorporate, then press the potatoes down to ensure they are as covered in the cheese sauce as much as possible. Cover with foil, then bake for 60-70 minutes or until all potatoes have cooked through. In the last 10 minutes, remove the foil or lid and sprinkle on the Parmesan cheese, then continue baking. Allow to rest for 10 minutes prior to serving.

Brussels Sprouts with Bacon

Prep Time: 10 Cook Time: 15 Recipe quantity: —

INGREDIENTS

- 6 strips of low-sodium bacon, diced
- 3 cups (10oz) frozen Brussels sprouts
- 3 tbsp butter
- 1 medium yellow onion (8oz), diced
- ½ tsp black pepper
- ½ tsp garlic powder

Nutrition Facts

Serving size	
Amount Per Serving	
Calories	**600**
	% Daily Value*
Total Fat 45g	**58%**
Saturated Fat 18g	**90%**
Trans Fat 0g	
Cholesterol 75mg	**25%**
Sodium 500mg	**22%**
Total Carbohydrate 27g	**10%**
Dietary Fiber 8g	**29%**
Total Sugars 8g	
Includes 0g Added Sugars	**0%**
Protein 26g	**52%**
Vitamin D 0mcg	0%
Calcium 98mg	8%
Iron 5mg	30%
Potassium 813mg	15%

*The % Daily Value (DV) tells you how much a nutrient in a serving of food contributes to a daily diet. 2,000 calories a day is used for general nutrition advice.

DIRECTIONS

Thaw the Brussels sprouts, or if preferred, steam in a saucepan for 5 minutes. Once thawed, roughly chop the Brussels sprouts. In a wide skillet, cook the bacon until just prior to crispy. Remove the bacon, then remove all but 1 tbsp of bacon fat from the skillet. Add the butter. Once melted, add the chopped Brussels sprouts and diced onion. Cook on medium-high heat until the edges of the Brussels sprouts begin to brown (~7-10 minutes), stirring often. Sprinkle with garlic powder and black pepper, stir, and cook for 1 additional minute prior to serving.

Buttered Potatoes

Prep Time: 25 Cook Time: 10 Recipe quantity: —

INGREDIENTS

- **1½lbs baby red potatoes**
- **1 tsp unsalted butter + 2 tbsp**
- **1 medium yellow onion (8oz), roughly chopped**
- **1 tbsp dried parsley**
- **½ tsp black pepper**
- **½ tsp garlic powder**

Nutrition Facts	
Serving size	
Amount Per Serving	
Calories	**860**
	% Daily Value*
Total Fat 28g	**36%**
Saturated Fat 9g	**45%**
Trans Fat 0g	
Cholesterol 35mg	**12%**
Sodium 10mg	**0%**
Total Carbohydrate 146g	**53%**
Dietary Fiber 11g	**39%**
Total Sugars 9g	
Includes 0g Added Sugars	**0%**
Protein 17g	**34%**
Vitamin D 0mcg	0%
Calcium 167mg	15%
Iron 9mg	50%
Potassium 3379mg	70%

*The % Daily Value (DV) tells you how much a nutrient in a serving of food contributes to a daily diet. 2,000 calories a day is used for general nutrition advice.

DIRECTIONS

In a saucepan, boil the potatoes for 20 minutes or until they collapse under light pressure. Drain, and remove the potatoes to a separate plate. In the same saucepan, melt 1 tbsp butter and cook the onion over medium heat until translucent (~5-7 minutes). Add the potatoes back to the pan along with the 2 tbsp butter, parsley, black pepper, and garlic powder. Stir to combine, then cook for 3 minutes before serving.

Buttermilk Biscuits

Prep Time: 20 Cook Time: 15 Recipe quantity:

INGREDIENTS

- **2 tsp lemon juice**
- **¾ cup milk**
- **2 cups all-purpose flour**
- **1 tbsp granulated sugar**
- **1 tbsp sodium-free baking powder**
- **6 tbsp cold unsalted butter, cut into ¼" cubes**
- **1 tbsp unsalted butter, melted**

Nutrition Facts

Serving size	
Amount Per Serving	
Calories	**1660**
	% Daily Value*
Total Fat 83g	**106%**
Saturated Fat 32g	**160%**
Trans Fat 0g	
Cholesterol 130mg	**43%**
Sodium 80mg	**3%**
Total Carbohydrate 198g	**72%**
Dietary Fiber 24g	**86%**
Total Sugars 21g	
Includes 0g Added Sugars	**0%**
Protein 30g	**60%**
Vitamin D 2mcg	10%
Calcium 1185mg	90%
Iron 8mg	45%
Potassium 2871mg	60%

*The % Daily Value (DV) tells you how much a nutrient in a serving of food contributes to a daily diet. 2,000 calories a day is used for general nutrition advice.

DIRECTIONS

Preheat the oven to 425°F. Create the buttermilk by mixing the lemon juice and milk in a small glass or bowl. Set aside while preparing the dry ingredients. In a large bowl, combine the flour, sugar, and baking powder, then stir to mix. Add the butter cubes to the flour mix, and with your hands, pinch the butter cubes within the flour until the flour has a 'crumb'-type appearance. Add the buttermilk and mix for about 15 seconds to incorporate. The batter will be sticky but should not be mixed excessively. With your hands, transfer the dough to a floured surface and knead for 30 seconds. Flatten the dough to 1" thick and cut out the biscuits (I use the top of a drinking glass to cut), reforming any leftover dough and cut additional biscuits until an unusable amount remains. Line the cut biscuits on a greased cookie sheet and bake for 13-15 minutes or until the tops become lightly browned. Prior to serving, brush the tops with the melted butter.

Cornbread

Prep Time: 15 Cook Time: 35 Recipe quantity:

INGREDIENTS

- ½ cup yellow cornmeal
- 1½ cups all-purpose flour
- 2/3 cup sugar
- 1 tbsp sodium-free baking powder
- 2 eggs
- 1¼ cups milk
- 3 tbsp unsalted butter, softened
- 1/3 cup canola oil
- 1 tbsp honey

Nutrition Facts	
Serving size	
Amount Per Serving	
Calories	2670
	% Daily Value*
Total Fat 128g	**164%**
Saturated Fat 28g	**140%**
Trans Fat 0g	
Cholesterol 460mg	**153%**
Sodium 270mg	**12%**
Total Carbohydrate 355g	**129%**
Dietary Fiber 21g	**75%**
Total Sugars 160g	
Includes 0g Added Sugars	**0%**
Protein 46g	**92%**
Vitamin D 5mcg	25%
Calcium 1395mg	110%
Iron 8mg	45%
Potassium 3280mg	70%

*The % Daily Value (DV) tells you how much a nutrient in a serving of food contributes to a daily diet. 2,000 calories a day is used for general nutrition advice.

DIRECTIONS

Preheat the oven to 350°F. In a medium bowl, combine the dry ingredients - cornmeal, flour, sugar, and baking powder, then stir to combine. In a separate bowl, beat the eggs with the milk, then add the remaining wet ingredients - butter, canola oil, and honey, then whisk again to combine. Pour the wet ingredients into the dry ingredient bowl and whisk until lumps are gone. Pour the batter into a greased, standard pie pan or 8"x8" baking dish. Bake 30 to 35 minutes or until a toothpick inserted into the center area of the pan comes out dry.

Fried Zucchini

Prep Time: 20 Cook Time: 20 Recipe quantity: ——

INGREDIENTS

- **2 cups canola or vegetable oil for frying**
- **4 medium-sized zucchini, peeled and ends removed**
- **2 cups all-purpose flour**
- **2 eggs**
- **½ cup milk**
- **3 cups unseasonsed breadcrumbs**
- **2 tbsp Parmesan cheese**

Nutrition Facts	
Serving size	
Amount Per Serving	
Calories	**2090**
	% Daily Value*
Total Fat 45g	**58%**
Saturated Fat 11g	**55%**
Trans Fat 0g	
Cholesterol 400mg	**133%**
Sodium 630mg	**27%**
Total Carbohydrate 354g	**129%**
Dietary Fiber 38g	**136%**
Total Sugars 26g	
Includes 0g Added Sugars	**0%**
Protein 76g	**152%**
Vitamin D 3mcg	15%
Calcium 322mg	25%
Iron 15mg	80%
Potassium 3268mg	70%

*The % Daily Value (DV) tells you how much a nutrient in a serving of food contributes to a daily diet. 2,000 calories a day is used for general nutrition advice.

DIRECTIONS

Slice the zucchini into ¼" thick slices. Prepare 3 dredging bowls - one with the flour, one with the egg and milk whisked together, and one with the breadcrumbs. Heat the oil to 350°F in a wide skillet. Dredge each slice in the flour, then the egg mixture, then the breadcrumbs. Place one batch of breaded zucchini in the oil at a time, cooking on each side for approximately 2 minutes or until the breadcrumbs turn a medium brown color. After cooking, transfer the zucchini to a wire rack or a plate lined with a paper towel. Sprinkle on the Parmesan cheese and serve while warm.

Fruit Salad

Prep Time: 15 Cook Time: 0 Recipe quantity:

INGREDIENTS

- **1 20oz can pineapple chunks**
- **4 cups Mandarin orange slices**
- **3 bananas, peeled and sliced**
- **2 cups blueberries**
- **2 cups strawberries, sliced**
- **3 medium peaches, sliced**
- **2 medium golden delicious apples, chopped**
- **1 cup (4oz) walnuts, chopped**
- **1 3.4oz box vanilla instant pudding mix**

Nutrition Facts

Serving size	
Amount Per Serving	
Calories	**2900**
	% Daily Value*
Total Fat 77g	**99%**
Saturated Fat 6g	**30%**
Trans Fat 0g	
Cholesterol 0mg	**0%**
Sodium 1310mg	**57%**
Total Carbohydrate 552g	**201%**
Dietary Fiber 72g	**257%**
Total Sugars 409g	
Includes 0g Added Sugars	**0%**
Protein 36g	**72%**
Vitamin D 0mcg	0%
Calcium 578mg	45%
Iron 12mg	70%
Potassium 5905mg	130%

*The % Daily Value (DV) tells you how much a nutrient in a serving of food contributes to a daily diet. 2,000 calories a day is used for general nutrition advice.

DIRECTIONS

Drain the pineapple juice into a small bowl, then in a large bowl add all remaining fruit ingredients and the walnuts. Stir to combine. Add the dry vanilla pudding mix to the pineapple juice and stir well to combine. Pour the juice and pudding mixture over the fruit, then stir to incorporate. Chill for 1 hour, then serve. Top with ice cream or whipped cream if desired.

Green Beans with Bacon

Prep Time: 5 Cook Time: 15 Recipe quantity: —

INGREDIENTS

- **2 (14.5oz) cans no-salt-added green beans, undrained**
- **2 slices low-sodium bacon, diced**
- **½ medium yellow onion (4oz), diced**
- **½ tsp black pepper**
- **1 tsp Parmesan**

Nutrition Facts

Nutrition Facts	
Serving size	
Amount Per Serving	
Calories	**230**
	% Daily Value*
Total Fat 4g	**5%**
Saturated Fat 2g	**10%**
Trans Fat 0g	
Cholesterol 10mg	**3%**
Sodium 280mg	**12%**
Total Carbohydrate 33g	**12%**
Dietary Fiber 8g	**29%**
Total Sugars 16g	
Includes 0g Added Sugars	**0%**
Protein 14g	**28%**
Vitamin D 0mcg	0%
Calcium 243mg	20%
Iron 6mg	35%
Potassium 482mg	10%

*The % Daily Value (DV) tells you how much a nutrient in a serving of food contributes to a daily diet. 2,000 calories a day is used for general nutrition advice.

DIRECTIONS

Pour the green beans into a medium saucepan. Heat to boiling, simmer for 5 minutes, then drain. While the beans are heating, cook the bacon with the onion in a small skillet, then drain. Add the cooked bacon and onion to the green beans and stir to combine. Sprinkle on the pepper and Parmesan and stir to mix, then serve.

Macaroni and Cheese

Prep Time: 5 Cook Time: 25 Recipe quantity:

INGREDIENTS

- 16 oz elbow noodles
- 8 tbsp unsalted butter
- ½ cup all-purpose flour
- 1½ tsp onion powder
- 1 tbsp yellow mustard
- 3 cups milk
- 2 cups shredded cheddar cheese

Nutrition Facts

Serving size	
Amount Per Serving	
Calories	**3940**
	% Daily Value*
Total Fat 192g	**246%**
Saturated Fat 95g	**475%**
Trans Fat 0g	
Cholesterol 465mg	**155%**
Sodium 1920mg	**83%**
Total Carbohydrate 435g	**158%**
Dietary Fiber 30g	**107%**
Total Sugars 44g	
Includes 0g Added Sugars	**0%**
Protein 142g	**284%**
Vitamin D 6mcg	30%
Calcium 2616mg	200%
Iron 18mg	100%
Potassium 2609mg	60%

*The % Daily Value (DV) tells you how much a nutrient in a serving of food contributes to a daily diet. 2,000 calories a day is used for general nutrition advice.

DIRECTIONS

Cook the elbow noodles according to package directions, then drain. In a large saucepan, melt the butter and then add in the flour, onion powder, and yellow mustard. Stir to combine, then cook over medium-high heat until the flour begins to turn a light brown color (~3-5 minutes). Then, begin to add in the milk slowly, whisking constantly to remove any flour lumps. Cook over medium heat until the sauce thickens (~5 minutes), then begin to add the cheese in batches, stirring constantly. Once the cheese is fully incorporated, stir in the elbow noodles. Serve immediately.

Mashed Potatoes

Prep Time: 20 Cook Time: 0 Recipe quantity:

INGREDIENTS

- **5 large Russet potatoes, skinned and chopped into 1" cubes**
- **¾ cup milk**
- **¾ cup sour cream**
- **3 tbsp unsalted butter**
- **1 tsp black pepper**

Nutrition Facts	
Serving size	
Amount Per Serving	
Calories	**1550**
	% Daily Value*
Total Fat 73g	**94%**
Saturated Fat 37g	**185%**
Trans Fat 0g	
Cholesterol 190mg	**63%**
Sodium 170mg	**7%**
Total Carbohydrate 205g	**75%**
Dietary Fiber 14g	**50%**
Total Sugars 22g	
Includes 0g Added Sugars	**0%**
Protein 33g	**66%**
Vitamin D 2mcg	10%
Calcium 558mg	45%
Iron 12mg	70%
Potassium 4880mg	100%

*The % Daily Value (DV) tells you how much a nutrient in a serving of food contributes to a daily diet. 2,000 calories a day is used for general nutrition advice.

DIRECTIONS

Place the potato cubes into a medium-sized soup pot and add enough water to cover them. Boil the potatoes for 15 minutes or until they collapse under medium pressure. Once ready, drain the potatoes and return them to the same pot. Using a hand blender, begin to blend the potatoes while slowly incorporating the milk and butter. Once relatively smooth, add in the sour cream and black pepper and then blend for an additional 15 seconds. If the potatoes are still too thick (depending on their initial size), add equal parts of sour cream and milk until the desired consistency is achieved.

Onion Rings

Prep Time: 15 Cook Time: 20 Recipe quantity: —

INGREDIENTS

- **2 cups canola or vegetable oil for frying**
- **1 medium (8oz) yellow onion, cut into individual rings**
- **1 cup all-purpose flour**
- **1 tsp sodium-free baking powder**
- **3 eggs, beaten**
- **½ cup milk**
- **2 cups breadcrumbs, crushed**

Nutrition Facts	
Serving size	
Amount Per Serving	
Calories	1430
	% Daily Value*
Total Fat 47g	**60%**
Saturated Fat 11g	**55%**
Trans Fat 0g	
Cholesterol 575mg	**192%**
Sodium 410mg	**18%**
Total Carbohydrate 199g	**72%**
Dietary Fiber 17g	**61%**
Total Sugars 18g	
Includes 0g Added Sugars	**0%**
Protein 52g	**104%**
Vitamin D 4mcg	20%
Calcium 580mg	45%
Iron 9mg	50%
Potassium 1534mg	35%

*The % Daily Value (DV) tells you how much a nutrient in a serving of food contributes to a daily diet. 2,000 calories a day is used for general nutrition advice.

DIRECTIONS

In a wide skillet, heat the oil to 350°F. While heating, set up three bowls to hold the dredging material - one with the flour and baking powder, one with the beaten eggs and milk mixed together, and one with the breadcrumbs. Dredge the onion rings in the flour, then the egg mixture, then the breadcrumbs. Press the breadcrumbs onto the onion to help increase the adhesion. Fry the onion rings for approximately 2 minutes per side until the breadcrumbs are golden brown. Once a batch is done frying, move the onion rings to a wire rack for cooling.

Potato Salad

Prep Time: 30 Cook Time: 0 Recipe quantity:

INGREDIENTS

- 2lbs red potatoes, cut into 1" cubes
- ¾ cup mayonnaise
- ¼ cup sweet relish
- 1 tbsp apple cider vinegar
- 2 tsp yellow mustard
- 1 tsp granulated sugar
- 1 tsp black pepper
- ½ cup (2oz) celery, diced
- ¼ cup (1oz) green onion, sliced
- 4 hardboiled eggs, cooled and chopped

Nutrition Facts

Serving size

Amount Per Serving	
Calories	**2220**
	% Daily Value*
Total Fat 155g	**199%**
Saturated Fat 26g	**130%**
Trans Fat 0g	
Cholesterol 860mg	**287%**
Sodium 1730mg	**75%**
Total Carbohydrate 180g	**65%**
Dietary Fiber 15g	**54%**
Total Sugars 22g	
Includes 20g Added Sugars	**40%**
Protein 43g	**86%**
Vitamin D 4mcg	20%
Calcium 311mg	25%
Iron 20mg	110%
Potassium 4363mg	90%

*The % Daily Value (DV) tells you how much a nutrient in a serving of food contributes to a daily diet. 2,000 calories a day is used for general nutrition advice.

DIRECTIONS

Boil the potato cubes in water for 20 minutes or until they collapse under pressure. Once cooked, drain and then chill the potatoes. Make the salad dressing by mixing the mayonnaise, relish, cider vinegar, mustard, sugar, and black pepper in a small bowl. When the potatoes have cooled, mix them with the dressing in a medium-sized bowl until fully coated. Gently mix in the celery, onion, and eggs. Serve chilled.

Risotto

Prep Time: 5 Cook Time: 30 Recipe quantity:

INGREDIENTS

- **1 tbsp olive oil**
- **½ medium yellow onion (4oz), diced**
- **1 cup dry white arborio rice**
- **½ tsp garlic powder**
- **½ cup white wine**
- **5 cups sodium-free chicken broth**
- **¼ cup Parmesan cheese**

Nutrition Facts

Serving size	
Amount Per Serving	
Calories	**1090**
	% Daily Value*
Total Fat 20g	**26%**
Saturated Fat 6g	**30%**
Trans Fat 0g	
Cholesterol 30mg	**10%**
Sodium 300mg	**13%**
Total Carbohydrate 165g	**60%**
Dietary Fiber 1g	**4%**
Total Sugars 8g	
Includes 5g Added Sugars	**10%**
Protein 26g	**52%**
Vitamin D 0mcg	0%
Calcium 211mg	15%
Iron 0mg	0%
Potassium 1999mg	45%

*The % Daily Value (DV) tells you how much a nutrient in a serving of food contributes to a daily diet. 2,000 calories a day is used for general nutrition advice.

DIRECTIONS

In a wide skillet, heat the olive oil over medium-high heat. Add the onion and cook until the onion begins to turn translucent (~5-7 minutes). Add the rice to the skillet and cook, stirring constantly, just until the rice begins to turn a light brown color. Add the garlic powder and wine and continue to cook, stirring often, until the wine is absorbed. Then begin to add the chicken broth to the pan in ½ cup increments, stirring often, adding more broth as the previous addition gets absorbed. Continue adding broth until the rice is tender and no liquid remains in the pan (you may not need all 5 cups of broth). Turn off the heat and stir in the Parmesan cheese. Allow to rest 5 minutes before serving.

Spanish Rice

Prep Time: 20 Cook Time: 15 Recipe quantity:

INGREDIENTS

- **2½ cups sodium-free chicken broth**
- **1¼ cups long-grain rice**
- **1 (14.5oz) can no-salt-added diced tomatoes, drained**
- **1 tbsp unsalted butter**
- **2 tsp sodium-free chili powder**
- **1 tsp cumin**
- **1 tsp dried oregano**
- **½ tsp garlic powder**

Nutrition Facts

Serving size	
Amount Per Serving	
Calories	**980**
	% Daily Value*
Total Fat 11g	**14%**
Saturated Fat 4g	**20%**
Trans Fat 0g	
Cholesterol 15mg	**5%**
Sodium 45mg	**2%**
Total Carbohydrate 204g	**74%**
Dietary Fiber 3g	**11%**
Total Sugars 12g	
Includes 2g Added Sugars	**4%**
Protein 21g	**42%**
Vitamin D 0mcg	0%
Calcium 34mg	2%
Iron 2mg	10%
Potassium 1696mg	35%

*The % Daily Value (DV) tells you how much a nutrient in a serving of food contributes to a daily diet. 2,000 calories a day is used for general nutrition advice.

DIRECTIONS

In a large bowl, rinse the rice by adding the rice and ample water, stirring the rice, then draining the water. Bring the chicken stock to a boil in a saucepan and then add the rinsed rice. Cover and cook at medium-low heat for approximately 30 minutes, or until the rice has absorbed most of the liquid. Add the remaining ingredients, stir to combine, and cook covered over medium heat for 5 minutes.

Sweet Corn

Prep Time: 2 Cook Time: 1 Recipe quantity: —

INGREDIENTS

- **2 (15oz) cans no-salt-added sweet corn, undrained**
- **1 tbsp olive oil**
- **2 tbsp unsalted butter, cut into slices**
- **½ tsp black pepper**

Nutrition Facts

Serving size	
Amount Per Serving	
Calories	**460**
	% Daily Value*
Total Fat 36g	**46%**
Saturated Fat 10g	**50%**
Trans Fat 0g	
Cholesterol 30mg	**10%**
Sodium 105mg	**5%**
Total Carbohydrate 29g	**11%**
Dietary Fiber 7g	**25%**
Total Sugars 14g	
Includes 0g Added Sugars	**0%**
Protein 7g	**14%**
Vitamin D 0mcg	0%
Calcium 217mg	15%
Iron 6mg	35%
Potassium 420mg	8%

*The % Daily Value (DV) tells you how much a nutrient in a serving of food contributes to a daily diet. 2,000 calories a day is used for general nutrition advice.

DIRECTIONS

Pour the corn into a medium saucepan. Heat to boiling, simmer for 5 minutes, then drain. Over medium heat, add the olive oil, butter, and pepper to the corn. Stir gently until the butter has melted, then serve.

Desserts

Apple Crisp

Prep Time: 20 Cook Time: 45 Recipe quantity:

INGREDIENTS

- **5 tart apples, peeled, cored, and sliced**
- **2 tbsp sugar**
- **2 tbsp brown sugar**
- **1½ tsp cinnamon**
- **¼ tsp nutmeg**
- **2 tbsp unsalted butter, melted**

Topping

- **¾ cup + 2 tbsp all-purpose flour**
- **6 tbsp rolled oats**
- **7 tbsp granulated sugar**
- **½ cup brown sugar**
- **12 tbsp unsalted butter, cut into ½" cubes**

Nutrition Facts

Serving size	
Amount Per Serving	
Calories	**3410**
	% Daily Value*
Total Fat 157g	**201%**
Saturated Fat 56g	**280%**
Trans Fat 0g	
Cholesterol 210mg	**70%**
Sodium 10mg	**0%**
Total Carbohydrate 487g	**177%**
Dietary Fiber 39g	**139%**
Total Sugars 342g	
Includes 0g Added Sugars	**0%**
Protein 19g	**38%**
Vitamin D 0mcg	0%
Calcium 73mg	6%
Iron 8mg	45%
Potassium 1796mg	40%

*The % Daily Value (DV) tells you how much a nutrient in a serving of food contributes to a daily diet. 2,000 calories a day is used for general nutrition advice.

DIRECTIONS

Preheat the oven to 350°F. In a 1-2 quart oven-safe dish, mix the apple slices with the sugar, brown sugar, cinnamon, and nutmeg, and allow to rest for 10 minutes. Meanwhile, in a separate bowl mix the flour, oats, sugar, and brown sugar, then add the butter cubes and mix to incorporate, slightly crushing the cubes with your fingers while mixing so that large crumbs are formed in the dry topping. Pour the melted butter over the apple slices, then sprinkle the topping over the apples. Bake for about 45 minutes, or until cooked through. For best flavor, serve while warm.

Banana Bread

Prep Time: 20 Cook Time: 60 Recipe quantity:

INGREDIENTS

- **2/3 cup brown sugar**
- **½ cup unsalted butter, slightly softened**
- **2 eggs**
- **1¾ cup ripened bananas, mashed**
- **1 tsp vanilla extract**
- **2 cups all-purpose flour**
- **2 tsp sodium-free baking powder**
- **1 tsp ground cinnamon**
- **2 tbsp diced walnuts**

Nutrition Facts	
Serving size	
Amount Per Serving	
Calories	2900
	% Daily Value*
Total Fat 107g	**137%**
Saturated Fat 37g	**185%**
Trans Fat 0g	
Cholesterol 490mg	**163%**
Sodium 150mg	**7%**
Total Carbohydrate 435g	**158%**
Dietary Fiber 37g	**132%**
Total Sugars 201g	
Includes 0g Added Sugars	**0%**
Protein 42g	**84%**
Vitamin D 2mcg	10%
Calcium 739mg	60%
Iron 12mg	70%
Potassium 3893mg	80%

*The % Daily Value (DV) tells you how much a nutrient in a serving of food contributes to a daily diet. 2,000 calories a day is used for general nutrition advice.

DIRECTIONS

Preheat the oven to 350°F. In a large bowl, beat the brown sugar and softened butter with a hand mixer for one minute. Then, add the eggs, bananas, and vanilla extract and mix on low for 30 seconds or until well incorporated. In a separate medium-sized bowl, mix the flour, baking powder, and cinnamon. Once mixed, add the wet ingredients to the flour mixture and stir until just incorporated, then fold in the walnuts. Pour the batter into a greased 9"x5" loaf pan and bake for 1 hour or until a toothpick inserted into the center comes out dry. Allow to cool before serving.

Cherry Mash

Prep Time: 10 Cook Time: 0 Recipe quantity:

INGREDIENTS

- 1 20 oz can cherry pie filling
- 1 14oz can sweetened condensed milk
- 1 cup (4oz) walnuts, chopped
- 1 20oz can crushed pineapple, drained
- 1 8oz container whipped topping
- 2½ cups mini-marshmallows

Nutrition Facts

Serving size

Amount Per Serving	
Calories	**3950**
	% Daily Value*
Total Fat 127g	**163%**
Saturated Fat 46g	**230%**
Trans Fat 0g	
Cholesterol 100mg	**33%**
Sodium 570mg	**25%**
Total Carbohydrate 649g	**236%**
Dietary Fiber 20g	**71%**
Total Sugars 521g	
Includes 374g Added Sugars	**748%**
Protein 55g	**110%**
Vitamin D 0mcg	0%
Calcium 1020mg	80%
Iron 8mg	45%
Potassium 3295mg	70%

*The % Daily Value (DV) tells you how much a nutrient in a serving of food contributes to a daily diet. 2,000 calories a day is used for general nutrition advice.

DIRECTIONS

In a large bowl, mix all ingredients thoroughly, then chill for 2 hours. As an alternate, spread the mixed ingredients into a 9"x13" baking dish and freeze. Thaw for one hour before serving.

Appendix

Appendix A: Recipe Classification

On the next few pages are a list of all recipes in this book along with a set of recipe indicators to help in your recipe selection process. The indicators I have chosen to include for this section are outlined as follows:

Vegetarian:	There are many variations of vegetarian diets. For this selection I have chosen to focus on ovo-lacto vegetarian diets; therefore, recipes marked as "vegetarian" do not include any meat product (e.g. beef, chicken, fish, or stock) but may contain egg or milk
Low-carb:	Low-carb diets emphasize a reduction in sugar, a form of carbohydrate. Carbohydrate comes in all forms that range from simple granulated sugar to pasta. Typically, low-carb diets are based upon serving size. Because dishes in this cookbook are outlined as 'entire recipes', it requires a judgment call on how much carbohydrate is allowed. Recipes in this section marked as 'low carb' include less than 100g of carbohydrate for the recipe, but it is ultimately up to you to determine whether the listed amount is an acceptable level of carbohydrate. *Note*: Several additional recipes can classify as low carb by making subtle ingredient modifications
Low-cholesterol:	Saturated fat consumption has a bigger effect on raising your cholesterol than does consuming cholesterol. Those recipes marked as 'low cholesterol' on the next pages have a relatively low saturated fat content in proportion to the size of the recipe (i.e. less than 5g of saturated fat for minimal and medium-sized recipes, less than 10g for medium-large meals, and less than 20g for large recipes) and may be of consideration for those attempting to lower their cholesterol levels.
Author Favorite:	My own personal favorite recipes whether due to convenience or frequent cravings.
Kid Favorite:	Recipes that my kids request most often.

	Vegetarian	Low-Carb	Low-Cholesterol	Author Favorite	Family Favorite
Baked Chicken Tetrazzini					
Baked Chicken Wings				x	
Beef Enchiladas					
Beef Fried Rice					
Beef Jerky		x			
Beef & Potato Stroganoff				x	x
Beef Stew					
Beef Stir Fry					
Beef Tips		x			
Bierocks				x	x
Broccoli Chicken Pasta					
Catfish Nuggets					
Cheeseburger Macaroni					
Cheesy Beef Pasta					
Chicken and Dumplings					
Chicken Carbonara					
Chicken Cheese Nuggets		x			
Chicken Fried Steak					
Chicken Noodle Soup			x		x
Chicken Pasta			x		
Chicken Salad		x			
Chicken Stew			x		
Chicken Stir Fry			x		
Chicken Tetrazzini					
Chili				x	x
Chili-2					
Corn Chowder		x			
Cottage Pie					
Creamy Pasta					
Creamy Pork Chops		x			
Fajita					
Fettuccini Alfredo					
Fried Chicken					
Garden Pasta	x				
Garlic Pasta	x		x		
Goulash					

	Vegetarian	Low-Carb	Low-Cholesterol	Author Favorite	Family Favorite
Goulash-2					
Green Bean Beef					
Ground Beef Ramen				x	
Hamburger Patty		x			
Lasagna					
Lemon Pepper Chicken					
Meatballs		x		x	
Meatloaf					
Mexican Casserole					
Minestrone					
Mongolian Beef Ramen					
Nachos		x		x	x
One Pot Pasta	x		x		
Parmesan Chicken					
Parmesan Chicken Pasta					
Parmesan Pasta					
Parmesan Pasta with Peas	x				
Pasta Primavera	x				
Patty Melt		x		x	
Pizza				x	x
Poppy Seed Pasta					
Pork Chops				x	
Pork Ribs					
Potato Skins					
Potato Soup					
Pulled Pork		x			
Quesadillas					
Roast					
Roasted Chicken with Veg		x			
Salisbury Steak		x			
Sheet pan Nachos					
Sloppy Joe					
Smothered Potato					
Spaghetti with Meat Sauce			x	x	x
Spinach Frittata		x			
Steak Bites		x			
Stroganoff-1					

	Vegetarian	Low-Carb	Low-Cholesterol	Author Favorite	Family Favorite
Stroganoff-2					
Stuffed Peppers					
Swiss Steak		x			
Taco Chili					
Tangy Chicken Wings					
Vegetable Beef Stew		x		x	x
Belgian Waffles	x			x	x
French Toast	x	x	x	x	x
Omelet Bowl		x			
Apple Crisp				x	
Cherry Mash				x	x
Au Gratin Potatoes					
Banana Bread					
Brussels Sprouts with Bacon		x		x	
Butter Potatoes	x		x		
Buttermilk Biscuits	x				
Cornbread	x				x
Fried Zucchini	x			x	x
Fruit Salad	x		x	x	
Green Beans with Bacon		x	x		
Macaroni and Cheese	x				
Mashed Potatoes	x				
Onion Rings	x				
Potato Salad	x				
Risotto			x		
Spanish Rice			x		
Sweet Corn	x	x			

Appendix B. Sodium Values for Selected Ingredients

Sodium values per unit of measure for a variety of ingredients used in this cookbook. Note: NSA = no salt added

Ingredient	Measure		Sodium (mg)
Bacon, Reduced Sodium	2	slices	150
Beans, Black NSA canned	1/2	cup	0
Beans, Pinto NSA canned	1/2	cup	5
Breadcrumbs, unseasoned	1/2	cup	35
Broth, beef, sodium free	1	cup	0
Broth, chicken, sodium free	1	cup	0
Cheese, cheddar shredded	1/4	cup	170
Cheese, Mozzarella shredded	1/4	cup	190
Cheese, parmesan grated	1	tbsp	75
Cheese, Swiss sliced	1	slice	40
Cheese, Swiss shredded	1/4	cup	55
Cheese, Ricotta	1/4	cup	55
Cherry pie filling	1/3	cup	15
Chiles, diced green	1/2	cup	15
Chips, Tortilla Unsalted	1	cup	10
Condensed Milk	2	tbsp	35
Cool Whip	2	tbsp	0
Corn, NSA canned	1/2	cup	15
Cream, Heavy Whipping	1	tbsp	5
Green beans, NSA canned	1/2	cup	15
Ground beef, chuck	4	oz	75
Ketchup, sodium-free	1	tbsp	0
Mayonnaise	1	tbsp	70
Milk, whole	1	cup	105
Mustard, Yellow	1	tsp	80
Sour cream	2	tbsp	15
Soy sauce	1	tbsp	55
Tomato Paste	2	tbsp	20
Tomato Sauce	1/4	cup	10

Tomatoes, diced, NSA canned	1/2	cup	15
Tortillas, corn	1	each	10
Vanilla pudding mix	1/4	pkg	320
Worcestershire sauce	1	tsp	60

Other Books By Mark Knoblauch

For more information about many of the topics covered in this book, please check out the following book:

Living Low Sodium: A guide for understanding our relationship with sodium and how to be successful in adhering to a low-sodium diet

For more information on Ménière's disease, please check out:

Overcoming Ménière's: How changing your lifestyle can change your life

Image Credits:

Figure 1: W.Y.Sunshine/shutterstock.com
Figure 2: MSVivienne/shutterstock.com
Figure 3: FDA.gov *Nutrition Facts Label Images for Download*

Recipe Quantity labels: stockvectorsillustrations/shutterstock.com

www.ingramcontent.com/pod-product-compliance
Lightning Source LLC
LaVergne TN
LVHW081251100826
845148LV00009B/1193

* 9 7 8 1 7 3 3 3 2 1 0 3 7 *